THE GOOD
Web Site
GUIDE 2001

THE GOOD
Web Site
GUIDE 2001

GRAHAM EDMONDS

ORION

First published in 2000 by Orion Media
An imprint of Orion Books Ltd
Orion House, 5 Upper St Martin's Lane,
London WC2H 9EA

A CIP catalogue record for this book is
available from the British Library.

ISBN 0 75283 811 3

Designed by Staziker Jones, Cardiff

Printed by Clays Ltd, St Ives plc

Introduction

So what's all the fuss about the internet? What use is the world wide web anyway? Well it's certainly changed my life as it has that of many other people. How?

Being more aware of my finances (**www.thisismoney.com**), monitoring my phone usage (**www.bt.com**), getting deals on holidays (**www.a2btravel.co.uk**), having train tickets delivered to my home (**www.thetrainline.co.uk**), buying presents for my nephews (**www.etoys.co.uk**) or for myself (**www.shopsmart.co.uk**), my home (**www.bluedeco.co.uk**), or for my girlfriend (**www.rigbyandpeller.com**), and I've even got someone to do the shopping for me (**www.ybag.co.uk**).

I've tried new foods (**www.bluemango.co.uk**), bought an antique from an auction (**www.icollector.co.uk**), arranged a visit to a New York art gallery (**www.moma.org**) and bought a poster or two (**www.artrepublic.com**).

Knowing about MP3 (a widely available program that allows you to download sound) has rekindled my interest in music (**www.real.com**) and I can share it with others (**www.napster.com**). I'm better informed about films: what's on, when and where (**www.popcorn.co.uk**) and I spend less time watching rubbish on television.

My sports knowledge (**www.sports.com**) has improved, and I feel I know more about what's going on in the world (**http://news.bbc.co.uk**).

My garden looks better too (**www.oxalis.co.uk**) as I have a better understanding of what plants grow well in my area (**http://fff.nhm.ac.uk/fff**).

I've helped friends find a better job (**www.stepstone.co.uk**) and a new house (**www.propertyfinder.co.uk**).

At work, I've found the number of someone who owed us money (**www.yell.co.uk**), collected company information (**www.ft.com**), obtained a great deal of specialist data and made contact with new suppliers.

Using the internet does not need to take over your life but it can greatly enhance it. I can really indulge my interests, be informed and experience things I've not experienced before. It's saved me time and money.

This book is designed to help you quickly get to grips with what the internet has to offer. I have visited thousands of web sites covering a bewildering range of topics, but I have concentrated on what's useful and popular.

It is disappointing to find so few really well-designed web sites. Most sites are informative and do the job but really entertaining sites, those that make you want to go back for more, are rare. Surprisingly few have that genuine "wow" factor. Hopefully, as access to the internet becomes to all intents and purposes "free" in this country and people use it more and more, good design and customer awareness will improve and web sites will become more inspired.

As a start here's my top ten of the best-designed and most user-friendly sites (in no particular order):

www.thetrainline.com (Order your train tickets)

www.go-fly.co.uk (Go Airlines)

www.metmuseum.org (Metropolitan Museum in New York)

www.3fatchicks.com (Dieting and health with attitude)

www.scoot.co.uk (Finding people, businesses or what's on)

www.shopsmart.co.uk (The best shops reviewed)

www.google.com (The fastest search engine)

www.jungle.co.uk (Music, computers and movies)

www.netradio.com (Music with a difference)

www.zoom.co.uk (Lifestyle with style)

There are more, but these are examples of sites with a special something that makes you want to come back and use them again. Web site designers who want our loyalty should take note and make their own sites similarly impressive.

USING THE LIST

Ratings

ORIGIN UK
SPEED ✓✓✓✓✓
INFO ✓✓✓✓✓
VALUE ✓✓✓✓✓
EASE ✓✓✓✓✓

✓ = slow/poor   ✓✓✓✓✓ = fast/good

Speed – Some sites take ages to download and use. This gives an indication of what you can expect from the site in question. During the course of preparing the book I visited each site at least 3 times. All the work was done on the same PC using the same service provider.

Info – This gives you a gauge of how much information is available, with respect to how much you are entitled to expect. It's also a measure of the number and quality of links they provide.

Value – Value for money. The more ✓s the better value you can expect. In some cases it's just not quantifiable, and has been omitted.

Ease – This is intended to give an indication of how easy the site is to use. Is it logical, easy to navigate or well signposted?

Origin – It's not always obvious where the site originates. This can be important, especially when you are buying from abroad. There may be restrictions or tax that isn't obvious at the time. Also information that is shown as general may apply to one part of the world and not another. For instance gardening advice on a US site will not necessarily apply to the UK.

Remember, I don't pretend to be a judge and jury, my ratings are just my opinion. Consequently, we have opened our own web site, **www.goodwebsiteguide.net**, which will be updated regularly with new site reviews, and I'd really appreciate your feedback. If you think there are sites I've missed or just want to give a view on a site in the book, e-mail me at info@goodwebsiteguide.net. This way next year's guide will be even better.

W?WT indicates a member of the Which? Trader Scheme. For more information see page 165 or visit their website at **www.which.net**

Tax – Beware of foreign taxes as not all foreign retailers include taxes in the quoted price. The US for instance quotes prices without tax and sales tax varies from state to state. Be aware and check before purchases, as shopping in a low-tax state can save you pounds.

Acknowledgements

I'd just like to end in thanking a few important people:

Firstly Orion, especially the sales team who I know have done a great job and Trevor Dolby who buys a good lunch and gave me the chance to get published.

Deborah Gray for patience and knowing how to conjugate a verb.

David Kohn for showing the way.

All my many friends and colleagues for their support and suggestions, especially Ian Moore for sheer enthusiasm.

Lastly to Michaela for love and shopping.

Aircraft

see Transport

Airlines

see Travel

Antiques & Collectibles

The internet is a great place to learn about antiques, it's also full of specialist sites run by fanatical collectors. If you want to take the risk of buying over the net then the best prices are found on the big auction sites such as Ebay and icollector.

www.antiquesworld.co.uk

FOR EVERYONE WITH AN INTEREST IN ANTIQUES AND COLLECTIBLES

ORIGIN UK	Catch up on the latest news, obtain details
SPEED ✓✓	on major fairs and events, book a course or indulge
INFO ✓✓✓✓✓	your interests by linking to a specialist on-line
EASE ✓✓✓	retailer or club. You can't buy from
	this site but the links and information are
	very good.

www.antiquesroadshow.co.uk

NO VALUATIONS JUST INFORMATION

ORIGIN UK	Nothing to do with the BBC, this site offers a
SPEED ✓✓	searchable directory to the UK's antiques and
INFO ✓✓✓✓	collectibles web sites. There is quality information
EASE ✓✓✓	about local auctions, shops and fairs and there is an
	excellent book section affiliated to Amazon. The site
	is very slow.

www.antiques-web.co.uk/fairs.html
DIRECTORY OF ANTIQUES FAIRS

ORIGIN UK	Simply lists antiques and collectors fairs in date
SPEED ✓✓	order with links to organiser's web sites, where
INFO ✓✓✓✓	available.
EASE ✓✓✓✓	

www.dmgantiquefairs.com
FOR THE LARGEST ANTIQUES FAIRS

ORIGIN UK	DMG run the largest fairs in the UK. Their attractive
SPEED ✓✓✓	site gives details of each fair, including dates, location
INFO ✓✓✓✓	and local tourist information.
EASE ✓✓✓✓	

www.worldcollectersnet.com
BY COLLECTORS FOR COLLECTORS

ORIGIN UK	If there's a market for it, it's here. Collectibles in all
SPEED ✓✓✓✓	shapes and sizes, the latest news, links to official sites,
INFO ✓✓✓	price guides and a newsletter. You can buy, sell or
VALUE ✓✓✓✓	trade at the Swap Shop, but beware of shipping costs
EASE ✓✓✓✓	and use your common sense.

Applemac Users

www.apple.com or www.uk.euro.apple.com
HOME OF THE ORIGINAL

ORIGIN US	Get the latest information and advances in Apple
SPEED ✓✓✓✓	computers at this beautifully designed site. You can
INFO ✓✓✓	buy from the Applestore but don't expect huge
VALUE ✓✓✓✓	discounts, although they do offer finance deals.
EASE ✓✓✓✓	

www.macwarehouse.co.uk
GREAT PRICES ON MACS

ORIGIN UK	Part of the Microwarehouse group, they specialise in
SPEED ✓✓✓	mail order supply with a reputation for excellent
INFO ✓✓✓✓	service. Good prices and a wide range make this a
VALUE ✓✓✓✓	good first port of call if you need a new PC or an
EASE ✓✓✓	upgrade.

www.macintouch.com
THE ORIGINAL MAC NEWS AND INFORMATION SITE

ORIGIN US	If you have a Mac then this is the site for you. It has
SPEED ✓✓✓	lots of information, bug fixes and software to down-
INFO ✓✓✓✓✓	load, but it is a little overwhelming and it takes a
EASE ✓✓	while to get your bearings. Once you've done that,
	for the Mac user this is invaluable.

Appliances

see Electrical Goods

Art & the Arts

One of the best things about the internet is the ability to show-case things that otherwise would be quite obscure or inaccessible. Working artists can show their wares to excellent effect, and we can now "visit" some of the world's great galleries and museums. Here are the best sites for posters, on-line galleries, museums, exhibitions, showcases for new talent and how to get the best clip-art for your own use.

Art – shops museums, galleries and exhibitions

www.artlex.com
THE VISUAL ARTS DICTIONARY

ORIGIN US
SPEED ✓✓
INFO ✓✓✓✓
EASE ✓✓✓

From abbozzo to zoomorphic, there are over 3000 definitions of art related terms with links to other sites and articles. It can be very slow to use, and some of the links aren't reliable.

http://wwar.com
THE WORLD-WIDE ART RESOURCE

ORIGIN US
SPEED ✓✓✓
INFO ✓✓✓✓✓
EASE ✓✓✓✓✓

This is an effective search vehicle with links to artists, exhibitions, galleries and museums. There are two main sections:
1. Services: art news, e-postcards, classified ads, young artist's CVs.
2. Visual: links to museums, artists, galleries, jobs and suppliers; also to performing arts, antiques, films and architectural sites.

www.design-council.org.uk
PROMOTING THE EFFECTIVE USE OF DESIGN

ORIGIN UK
SPEED ✓✓✓
INFO ✓✓✓
EASE ✓✓✓✓

This site effectively promotes the work of the design council through access to their archives of articles on design and details of their work with government; also gives feedback on design issues.

www.artguide.org
THE ART LOVER'S GUIDE TO BRITAIN AND IRELAND

ORIGIN UK
SPEED ✓✓✓
INFO ✓✓✓✓
EASE ✓✓✓✓

Organised by artist, region, exhibition or museum with more than 4500 listings in all. This site is easy to navigate with a good search engine and cross-referencing, making it easy to find out about events in a particular region; enhanced by annotated maps.

www.artplanet.com
THE INTERNET FINE ART DIRECTORY

ORIGIN US
SPEED ✓✓✓
INFO ✓✓✓
EASE ✓✓✓✓

Art Planet is a comprehensive on-line fine art directory, claiming over 11,000 entries. There are sections on artists, auction houses, galleries, libraries, museums, exhibitions, publishers, etc. However, it is biased towards the USA; its main strength is a list of good links to other art sites.

The major museums and galleries

www.tate.org.uk
THE ARCHETYPAL GALLERY SITE

ORIGIN UK
SPEED ✓✓
INFO ✓✓✓✓
VALUE ✓✓✓
EASE ✓✓✓✓

A real treat with good quality pictures, albeit a little serious. The site is divided into sections:

1. One for each Tate gallery, including what's on and what's coming.
2. The collection, which can easily be browsed or searched by artist.
3. The shop sells art related merchandise, but you must order by fax!
4. A forum for art chat and a feedback feature.
5. Notes about the sponsors.
6. Future plans for the galleries.
7. Details about touring exhibitions.

www.nationalgallery.org.uk
THE NATIONAL COLLECTION OF WESTERN EUROPEAN PAINTING

ORIGIN UK
SPEED ✓✓
INFO ✓✓✓✓✓
EASE ✓✓✓✓✓

Very comprehensive and similar to the academic style of the Tate site. Divided into five major sections:

1. The collection, very good quality pictures with notes on each one.

2. What's on and when.
3. Information on the gallery – how to get there etc.
4. What's new and coming.
5. A good search facility.

There is no on-line shop. For access to the all the Scottish National Galleries on a similar site, go to **www.natgalscot.ac.uk**

www.british-museum.ac.uk
BUILDING THE BRITISH MUSEUM

ORIGIN UK
SPEED ✓✓
INFO ✓✓✓✓✓
VALUE ✓✓
EASE ✓✓✓

A brand new attractive site with great graphics and pictures of exhibits. Excellent – pity there's not more of it.

www.npg.org.uk
THE NATIONAL PORTRAIT GALLERY

ORIGIN UK
SPEED ✓✓
INFO ✓✓✓✓✓
VALUE ✓✓
EASE ✓✓✓✓

With over 10,000 works on view, this is one of the biggest on-line galleries. It shows the most influential characters in British history portrayed by artists of their time. You can search by sitter or artist, and buy the print. The on-line shop offers options on print size, framing and delivery, including overseas.

www.moma.org
THE MUSEUM OF MODERN ART IN NEW YORK

ORIGIN US
SPEED ✓✓
INFO ✓✓✓✓✓
VALUE ✓✓
EASE ✓✓✓

This slow, but attractive site is split into six major areas:

1. The collection, with a selection of the best paintings.
2. What's on.
3. Education resources for teachers and pupils.
4. Details on becoming a member.
5. Visiting information.

6. The on-line store which is excellent for the unusual.

You need to install Shockwave for features such as the audio commentary on the paintings. Do browse the store as some products on sale are exclusive; members get discounts on items sold in the store. Delivery to the UK is expensive.

www.metmuseum.org

THE METROPOLITAN MUSEUM OF ART IN NEW YORK

ORIGIN US	A new and very stylish site, featuring lots of great
SPEED ✓✓	ideas. You can view any one of 3500 exhibits,
INFO ✓✓✓✓	become a member, or visit a special exhibition. The
VALUE ✓✓✓	shop offers a great range of products, many exclu-
EASE ✓✓✓✓	sive, and there's a handy gift finder service. Delivery
	costs to the UK depend on how much you spend.

www.uffizi.firenze.it/welcome.html

THE UFFIZI GALLERY IN FLORENCE

ORIGIN ITALY	It's the quality of the images of the paintings that
SPEED ✓✓✓	make this site stand out. They are superb and it's a
INFO ✓✓✓	shame that there are not more of them to view.
EASE ✓✓✓✓	Navigating is easy and quicker than most. There is
	also gallery information and a tour.

www.louvre.fr

FRANCE'S TREASURE HOUSE

ORIGIN FRANCE	Similar to the UK's National Gallery site:
SPEED ✓✓	1. You can take a virtual tour.
INFO ✓✓✓✓	2. View the collection.
VALUE ✓	3. Learn about its history.
EASE ✓✓✓✓	4. Check out the latest exhibitions and buy a ticket.
	5. The shop has interesting items and delivery to the UK is about £7.

www.guggenheim.org
VANGUARDS OF ARCHITECTURE AND CULTURE

ORIGIN US
SPEED ✓✓✓
INFO ✓✓✓✓
VALUE ✓✓
EASE ✓✓✓✓

There is the promise of a unique virtual museum, but while we wait, the other four; Berlin, Bilbao, Venice and New York can be visited here.

1. You can find out about exhibitions and collections, projects, tours, events and developmental programs.
2. Join. Membership entitles you to free entry and a store discount.
3. The store is stocked with a wonderful selection of unusual goods and gifts, and is not bad value. Delivery to the UK is around £20.

Ceramics

www.ukceramics.org
A CERAMICS SHOWCASE

ORIGIN UK
SPEED ✓✓✓
INFO ✓✓✓
EASE ✓✓✓✓✓

An excellent showcase site for new and established artists. It has beautiful pictures of the ceramics with good biographical information. The site enables you to contact each artist to buy their work.

www.claricecliff.com
THE FIRST LADY OF CERAMIC DESIGN

ORIGIN UK
SPEED ✓✓✓
INFO ✓✓✓✓✓
VALUE ✓✓
EASE ✓✓✓✓

A must for fans of Clarice Cliff pottery. There is information on auctions, biographical details, patterns, shapes; also a newsletter and forum for related chat. The site offers reproductions and related merchandise for sale.

Clip-art

www.clipart.com
THE PLACE TO START IF YOU NEED CLIP-ART

ORIGIN US
SPEED ✓✓✓
INFO ✓✓
EASE ✓✓✓✓

Links to over 500 clip-art sites but, using the good search facility, you should quickly find the perfect image. Although huge, this site is low on information. Many linked sites have free art for use, otherwise cost varies enormously depending on what you want. You can also try the very similar www.clipart.net as well.

Buying art

www.artrepublic.com
BOOKS, POSTERS AND WHAT'S ON WHERE

ORIGIN UK
SPEED ✓✓✓
INFO ✓✓✓
VALUE ✓✓✓
EASE ✓✓✓✓✓

A nicely designed, easy-to-use site, which features three sections:
1. Posters – choose from over 1500 posters, use the glossary of art terms or peruse artists biographical data.
2. Books – read reviews or select from over 30,000 books. Delivery costs £3 for anywhere.
3. What's on where – details of the latest exhibitions, competitions and travel information on London.

www.postershop.co.uk
FINE ART PRINTS AND POSTERS

ORIGIN UK
SPEED ✓✓✓
INFO ✓✓✓
VALUE ✓✓✓
EASE ✓✓✓✓

There are over 20,000 prints and posters available to buy, covering the work of over 100 artists. It has a good search facility which is a bit slow but easy-to-use. Delivery costs £5. See also www.onlineposters.com which is reviewed under www.artrepublic.co.uk above.

www.arthouse.uk.com
WATERCOLOURS ON THE WEB

ORIGIN	UK
SPEED	✓✓✓
INFO	✓✓✓
VALUE	✓✓
EASE	✓✓✓✓

Learn about the techniques of watercolours, go on a course, find out about exhibitions or book an artistic holiday. There are also several galleries devoted to artists with work for sale, and many pictures to view.

www.finedition.co.uk
FINE REPRODUCTIONS

ORIGIN	UK
SPEED	✓✓✓
INFO	✓✓✓
VALUE	✓✓
EASE	✓✓✓✓

If you're not a lottery winner and you fancy a Turner or a Constable, this is the site for you. Fine Edition will faithfully reproduce your favourite painting for £150 and upwards.

Astrology

www.astrology.com
GUIDANCE FOR THE NEW MILLENNIUM

ORIGIN	UK
SPEED	✓✓✓
INFO	✓✓✓✓
EASE	✓✓✓✓

A very comprehensive site offering free advice from the stars, you can buy a personalised reading and chart or just browse the more general horoscopes. You can find celebrity horoscopes too, and learn about the history and techniques of astrology.

www.russellgrant.co.uk
RUSSELL GRANT

ORIGIN	UK
SPEED	✓✓✓✓
INFO	✓✓✓
VALUE	✓✓
EASE	✓✓✓✓

Now is your chance to buy a horoscope from a real celebrity, costs range from £3.99 for a psychic reading to £23.99 for the 30-day works.

www.astrologer.com
THAT WHICH IS BEING DISCUSSED IS ALSO ARISING

ORIGIN UK
SPEED ✓✓✓✓
INFO ✓✓✓✓
EASE ✓✓✓✓

No, we didn't get it either, but this site has links to all the major astrological sites such as the Astrological Association, several on-line journals and the Matrix software site from which you can download programs that help you work out your own charts.

Astronomy

see Science and Space

Auctions & Classified Ads

Before using these sites be sure that you are aware of the rules and regulations surrounding the bidding process, and what your rights are as a seller or purchaser. If they are not properly explained during the registration process, use another site. They should also offer a return policy as well as insurance cover.

Whilst there are plenty of bargains available, not all the products on offer are cheaper than the high street or specialist vendor, it's very much a case of buyer beware. Having said that, once you're used to it, it can be fun and you can save a great deal of money.

www.ebay.co.uk
PERSON TO PERSON ON-LINE TRADING

ORIGIN UK
SPEED ✓✓✓
INFO ✓✓✓✓
VALUE ✓✓✓
EASE ✓✓✓✓

With over 3 million items you are likely to find what you want here. The emphasis is on collectibles and is strong on antiques of all sorts. There is a 24-hour support facility and automatic insurance cover on all items up to £120. Each person who has something to sell has been reviewed by previous clients, that way you can check up on their reliability.

www.ebid.co.uk
THE UK'S FINEST

ORIGIN UK	Claims to be the UK's finest on-line auction house,
SPEED ✓✓✓	and it is strong on design. The auctions can easily be
INFO ✓✓✓	accessed and browsed, although there is compara-
VALUE ✓✓✓	tively little on sale. Its strengths are in computing,
EASE ✓✓✓✓	electronics and music.

www.icollector.com
REDEFINING THE ART OF COLLECTING

ORIGIN US	Bringing together the wares of some 650 auction
SPEED ✓✓✓	houses, icollector is an ambitious project that works
INFO ✓✓✓✓	well. The emphasis is on art, antiques and
VALUE ✓✓✓	collectibles. It's American, so be sure that the auction
EASE ✓✓✓✓	house you're dealing with ships outside the USA.

www.qxl.com
A PAN-EUROPEAN AUCTION COMMUNITY

ORIGIN UK/EUROPE	This wide-ranging site offers anything from airline
SPEED ✓✓✓	tickets and holidays to cars, collectibles and
INFO ✓✓✓✓	electronics (in several languages). The quality of
VALUE ✓✓✓✓	merchandise seems better than most sites. Contains
EASE ✓✓✓✓	sections on killer bargains, £1 deals and star finds;
	there is a good search facility.

www.firedup.com
HEAVILY ADVERTISED AND OVER-HYPED?

ORIGIN UK	It's backed by Rupert Murdoch's News International
SPEED ✓✓✓	group, so expect the hype to continue. Still, it does
INFO ✓✓✓✓	offer a wide selection of things for sale and it's
VALUE ✓✓✓✓	particularly good for events and the unusual.
EASE ✓✓✓✓	

www.sothebys.com
QUALITY ASSURED, BUT JUST FOR THE CONNOISSEURS

You can bid in their on-line auctions, find out about

ORIGIN UK/US	
SPEED ✓✓✓	
INFO ✓✓✓	
VALUE ✓✓	
EASE ✓✓✓✓	

their normal auctions or enlist their help with one of the many extra services they offer. The emphasis here is on quality and the arts.

www.christies.com
FOR THOSE WITH DEEP WALLETS

ORIGIN UK	
SPEED ✓✓	
INFO ✓✓✓	
EASE ✓✓✓	

Christies have a slow site that tells you about them and their program of auctions. There is good information on how to buy and sell through them, but you can't carry out transactions from the site. The LotFinder service searches their auctions for that special item – for a fee.

www.exchangeandmart.co.uk
THOUSANDS OF ADS, UPDATED DAILY

ORIGIN UK	
SPEED ✓✓✓✓	
INFO ✓✓✓✓	
VALUE ✓✓✓✓	
EASE ✓✓✓✓	

Everything the paper has and more, great bargains on a massive range of goods found with a good search facility. It is split into 3 major sections:
1. Motoring, including cars, vans, number plates and finance.
2. Home, including holidays, DIY and gardening.
3. Products for small businesses, including computers.
You can place an ad or get involved with their on-line auctions.

www.loot.com
FREE ADS ON-LINE

ORIGIN UK	
SPEED ✓✓✓	
INFO ✓✓✓✓	
VALUE ✓✓✓✓	
EASE ✓✓✓	

Over 140,000 ads and over 3000 auctioned items make Loot a great place to go for a bargain. It's an interesting site to browse, with six major sections covering the usual classified ad subjects, supplemented by areas featuring jobs, accommodation and personals. Go to Loot café for a chat.

Babies

see Parenting

Beauty Products

see Fashion

The BBC

www.bbc.co.uk

THE UK'S MOST POPULAR WEB SITE

ORIGIN UK
SPEED ✓✓✓✓
INFO ✓✓✓✓✓
VALUE ✓✓✓
EASE ✓✓✓✓✓

The BBC's site deserves a special feature, it is a huge site with over 300 sections and it can be quite daunting. This review only scrapes the surface. The site is split into four major sections:

1. Find – an excellent search facility and a what's on guide.
2. Where you live – features from local TV and radio in Scotland, Wales, Northern Ireland and the English regions.
3. About the BBC – including a link to the BBC Shop.
4. Jump to – features sections that change, the key ones being:
   - News – keep up to date with the tickertape facility.
   - Weather – 1, 3 or 5 day forecasts and more.
   - Football – catch up on all the scores, news and gossip.
   - Education – a superb resource with features from many programs.
   - Entertainment – catch up with what's on in all the favourite BBC shows.
   - Health – the latest advice and news.
   - History – features from many history programs.

- Home and Garden – from pot plants to personal finance.
- Kids – the best of *Blue Peter*, *Newsround* and *Live & Kicking*; also info on the stars, have your say and games .
- Nature – from dinosaurs to frogspawn.
- Radio – find out what's on and visit the listening booth.
- Science – the latest inventions and discoveries.
- World Service – sections on world regions, with a live web cast and news bulletins.

As you'd expect the programming leads the tone of each section, and all have links to the BBC Web Guide that allows you to check on related links.

www.beeb.com
THE BBC'S SHOPPING GUIDE

ORIGIN UK
SPEED ✓✓✓✓
INFO ✓✓✓✓✓
VALUE ✓✓✓
EASE ✓✓✓✓

Using consumer programs to head each major section, the BBC attempt to offer the best advice and offers available on the web, using links to other on-line retailers.

1. Good Homes – advice on buying, selling and improving your home.
2. Gardeners World – tips, projects and more advice from the experts.
3. Top of the Pops – latest chart news.
4. Music magazine – for classical buffs.
5. Top Gear – where to buy and how to run your car.
6. Holiday – advice, ski guide and links.
7. Radio Times Comedy – visit the comedy zone.
8. BBC Shop – the best of BBC products, delivery charged according to what you spend.

You can also obtain full radio and TV listings by signing up to their ISP **www.freebeeb.com.**

Booksellers

Books were the first products to be sold in volume over the internet, and their success has meant that there are many on-line booksellers, all boast about how quick their service is and how many titles they can get. In the main, the basic service is the same wherever you go, just pick the bookshop that suits you.

www.amazon.co.uk
MORE THAN JUST A BOOKSTORE

ORIGIN	UK
SPEED	✓✓✓✓
INFO	✓✓✓✓
VALUE	✓✓✓
EASE	✓✓✓✓

Amazon is the leading on-line bookseller, and their formula of combining value with recommendation has been followed by most on-line stores. Amazon also sells music products and has an auction service. There are also zshops. Amazon act as a guarantor for the stores it recommends. For books, there are better prices elsewhere.

www.bol.com
THE EURO-BOOKSELLER

ORIGIN	UK/EUROPE
SPEED	✓✓✓
INFO	✓✓✓✓
VALUE	✓✓✓
EASE	✓✓✓✓

Owned by Bertlesmann, the German media giant, you can get access to books in seven European countries. Appeals to the true book lover, with lots of recommendations but few offers. The "books in the media" section provides day-by-day listing of books that were featured in TV programs, the press or on the radio.

www.waterstones.co.uk
ASK A BOOKSELLER

ORIGIN	UK
SPEED	✓✓✓✓
INFO	✓✓✓✓
VALUE	✓✓✓
EASE	✓✓✓✓

An extension of the high street store, this site is less fussy than Amazon and easier to use. If you are not sure of the book you want you can "ask a bookseller" and they will reply with a recommendation.

www.bookshop.co.uk

THE INTERNET BOOKSHOP

ORIGIN UK	Owned by WH Smith, this follows the usual internet
SPEED ✓✓✓✓	bookshop pattern, but it is slightly clearer with a
INFO ✓✓✓✓	variety of offers. Also sells videos, cds and games,
VALUE ✓✓✓✓	with links to other magazines and stationery.
EASE ✓✓✓✓	

www.thegoodbookguide.com

WHERE READERS FIND WRITERS AND
WRITERS FIND READERS

ORIGIN UK	A developing site with a nice amateurish feel. They
SPEED ✓✓✓	aim to promote good books by unbiased recommen-
INFO ✓✓✓✓✓	dation while promoting their magazine and awards.
EASE ✓✓✓	Readers rigorously assess each title before its inclu-
	sion in the guide and there are author profiles too.
	The shop offers some good discounts.

www.barnesandnoble.com

THE WORLD'S BIGGEST BOOKSELLER

ORIGIN UK	Barnes and Noble's site boasts more books than any
SPEED ✓✓✓	other on-line bookseller. In style it follows the other
INFO ✓✓✓	bookshops with an American bias. It has a good out-
VALUE ✓✓✓✓	of-print service and links up with www.BOL.com.
EASE ✓✓✓✓	

www.ottakars.co.uk

FREE DELIVERY TO STORE

ORIGIN UK	Clear and easy-to-use with some nice personal
SPEED ✓✓✓	touches; it offers the usual mix of range, recommen-
INFO ✓✓✓✓	dation, offers, events and competitions. You can
VALUE ✓✓✓✓	collect your order from the local store. **W?WT**
EASE ✓✓✓✓	

www.alphabetstreet.com
STREETS AHEAD

ORIGIN UK	Part of the Streets Online group, this site follows the
SPEED ✓✓✓	pattern for other bookshops. However, it offers free
INFO ✓✓✓✓	delivery in the UK. It also offers a cash back loyalty
VALUE ✓✓✓✓	scheme in conjunction with its other sites that sell
EASE ✓✓✓✓	music, games and DVDs.

www.bookpeople.co.uk
INCREDIBLE DISCOUNTS

ORIGIN UK	Offers a limited range of discounted books with up
SPEED ✓✓✓	to 75% off the r.r.p.; strong on children's titles but
INFO ✓✓✓	low on recommendations. Some books vary from
VALUE ✓✓✓✓✓	shop editions – using cheaper paper or in
EASE ✓✓✓✓	paperback. Delivery is free if you spend over £30,
	plus point-based loyalty scheme.

www.bibliomania.com
THE CLASSICS ON-LINE

ORIGIN US	A superb resource, Bibliomania have over 70 classic
SPEED ✓✓✓✓	novels, the complete works of Shakespeare, plus
INFO ✓✓✓✓✓	many classic reference works available for you to
VALUE ✓✓✓✓✓	print or download. You can search the entire site for
EASE ✓✓✓✓	quotes or for a specific book.

www.shakespeare.sk
COMPLETE WORKS

ORIGIN US	This is a straight forward site featuring the complete
SPEED ✓✓✓	writings of Shakespeare, including biographical details,
INFO ✓✓✓✓	and a glossary explaining the language of the time.
EASE ✓✓✓✓	

www.booklovers.co.uk
QUALITY SECOND-HAND BOOKS

ORIGIN UK	If you can't find the book you want, then this is
SPEED ✓✓✓✓	worth a try. There is an excellent search facility or
INFO ✓✓✓✓	you can leave them a request. They give a quote if
VALUE ✓✓✓✓	you want to sell a book or you can swap too.
EASE ✓✓✓✓	There's also an events listing for book fairs.

www.okukbooks.com
THE HOME OF BRITISH CHILDREN'S BOOKS

ORIGIN UK	OKUKBooks are specialists in children's books and
SPEED ✓✓✓	offer a comprehensive listing of what's available.
INFO ✓✓✓✓	Covers and blurb are shown for all titles. There are
VALUE ✓✓✓	sections on key characters and you can search by
EASE ✓✓✓	age range. Provide offers to schools and stuff to
	download for free. Could be much more fun and
	easier to navigate though.

www.audiobooks.co.uk
THE TALKING BOOKSHOP

ORIGIN UK	Specialists in books on tape, they have around 6000
SPEED ✓✓✓✓	titles in stock and can quickly get another 10,000.
INFO ✓✓✓✓	They also stock CDs but no MP3 yet. Search the site
VALUE ✓✓✓	by author or reader, as well as by title. There are
EASE ✓✓✓	some offers, but most stock is at full price with
	delivery being £2 per order.

Britain

see Travel

CDs

see Music

Cameras

see Photography and Electrical Goods

Cars

see Transport

Ceramics

see Art

Children's Sites, Toys, Games and Clothes

You can save pounds on children's clothes and toys by shopping over the net, its easy and the service is often excellent as the sites are put together by people who really care. The internet also offers another way to educate and entertain children, it fascinates them, and listed here are some of the best sites anywhere.

www.etoys.co.uk
FOCUSING ON CHILDREN

ORIGIN	UK/US
SPEED	✓✓✓✓
INFO	✓✓✓✓
VALUE	✓✓✓✓
EASE	✓✓✓✓

An excellent site for everything to do with buying for children, featuring not just toys, but also software, games and videos. Very easy-to-use and top of a recent customer service poll – there's even a price promise. Great for character merchandise and has a section that categorises toys by age. W?WT

www.funstore.co.uk
ON-LINE TOYS AND GAMES FOR THE UK

ORIGIN	UK
SPEED	✓✓✓
INFO	✓✓✓✓
VALUE	✓✓✓
EASE	✓✓✓✓

Funstore has brand names as well as the more traditional toys. The site is split into ten sections with several hundred items available to buy. Prices seem to be in line with or slightly below High Street. Delivery is £2.95 per order and gift-wrap at £1 per item.

www.hamleys.co.uk
FINEST TOY STORE IN THE WORLD

ORIGIN	UK
SPEED	✓✓
INFO	✓✓✓
VALUE	✓✓✓
EASE	✓✓✓

Hamleys is a slow site with many of the features of etoys with annoying graphics. The best thing about the site is the recommendations feature which helps you find the ideal toy for any child. Free delivery in the UK.

www.toysrus.co.uk
NOT JUST TOYS

ORIGIN	UK/US
SPEED	✓✓✓
INFO	✓✓✓✓
VALUE	✓✓✓✓
EASE	✓✓✓✓

Good site with all the key brands and "in" things you'd expect – you can even buy a mobile phone. Has links to key toy manufacturer's sites, and sister sites called www.discounttoys.co.uk for great bargains and www.babiesrus.co.uk. Delivery is £2.50 for the UK.

www.dawson-and-son.com
FOR TRADITIONAL WOODEN TOYS

ORIGIN	UK
SPEED	✓✓✓
INFO	✓✓✓
VALUE	✓✓
EASE	✓✓✓✓

Specialists in the art of making simple, traditional wooden toys, Dawson and Son offer a wide range of beautifully made items from rattles to sophisticated games. Delivery depends on the value and weight of order.

www.krucialkids.com

ALL ABOARD THE KRUCIAL KIDS EXPRESS

ORIGIN UK
SPEED ✓✓✓
INFO ✓✓✓✓
VALUE ✓✓✓
EASE ✓✓✓✓

Annoying name, but not an annoying site. It specialises in developmental toys for children 0 to 8 years old. Provides detailed information on the educational value of each of the 200 or so toys. The prices aren't bad either. Delivery is free if you spend over £60.

www.thepartystore.co.uk

SELLING FUN

ORIGIN UK
SPEED ✓✓
INFO ✓✓✓✓
VALUE ✓✓✓
EASE ✓✓✓✓

Not just for children, but there is an excellent kid's party section. They sell character outfits, themed tableware, masks, party boxes and all sorts of accessories. Delivery takes 4 working days and costs £2.95 but free if you spend £40 or more.

www.jojomamanbebe.co.uk

FASHIONABLE MOTHERS AND THEIR CHILDREN

ORIGIN UK
SPEED ✓✓✓
INFO ✓✓✓✓
VALUE ✓✓✓
EASE ✓✓✓✓

Excellent for everything from maternity wear and designer children's clothes to gifts for newborn babies. Also sections on toys, maternity products and special offers. All the designs are tested and they aim to be comfortable as well as fashionable. Delivery cost depends on how much you spend and the size of items bought. For babywear try www.overthemoon-babywear.co.uk while for older children www.tots2teens.co.uk is a good bet.

www.urchin.co.uk

SHOPPING WITH BRATTITUDE

Urchin has some 300 products available: cots and beds, bathtime accessories, bikes, clothes, for baby,

ORIGIN	UK
SPEED	✓✓✓
INFO	✓✓✓✓
VALUE	✓✓✓
EASE	✓✓✓✓

travel goods, toys and things for independent children who like to personalise their own rooms. They boast a sense of style and good design, and they succeed. Also have a bargains section. Delivery is £3.95 per order with a next day surcharge of £3.

Children's Books

see Books

www.mamamedia.com

THE PLACE FOR KIDS ON THE NET

ORIGIN	US
SPEED	✓✓✓
INFO	✓✓✓✓✓
EASE	✓✓✓✓

This versatile site has everything a child and parent would want, there is an excellent selection of interactive games, puzzles and quizzes, combined with a great deal of wit and fun. Its best feature is that it encourages children to communicate through the use of message boards and competitions while getting them to vote on what's important to them. There's a superb section on what's good on the net featuring some 2000 sites.

www.bonus.com

THE SUPERSITE FOR KIDS

ORIGIN	US
SPEED	✓✓✓
INFO	✓✓✓✓✓
EASE	✓✓✓✓✓

Excellent graphics and some genuinely good games make a visit to Bonus a treat for all ages. There are quizzes and puzzles, with sections offering a photo library, art resource and homework help. Access to the web is limited to a protected environment. Check out **www.kidsworld.com** and **www.wonka.com**, both are at least as good as Bonus.

www.yahooligans.com
THE WEB GUIDE FOR KIDS

ORIGIN US	Probably the most popular site for kids, yahooligans
SPEED ✓✓✓	offers parents safety and kids hours of fun. There
INFO ✓✓✓✓	are games, articles and features on the "in" charac-
EASE ✓✓✓✓	ters, education resources and sections on sport,
	science, computing and TV. It has an American bias.

www.kidsonline.co.uk
FOR KIDS BY KIDS

ORIGIN UK	Excellent graphics make this site stand out, and its
SPEED ✓✓	content is very good too; however it can be a little
INFO ✓✓✓	slow. Split into two sections for younger and older
EASE ✓✓✓✓	kids, there are reviews of favourite books, films and
	websites as well as a smattering of games.

www.citv.co.uk
CHILDREN'S ITV

ORIGIN UK	Keep up to date with your favourite programs and
SPEED ✓✓✓	talk to the stars of the shows. There's lots to do here
INFO ✓✓✓✓✓	including chat with fellow fans, play games, find
EASE ✓✓✓	something to do, enter a competition, e-mail a friend
	and join the club.

www.cartoonnetwork.co.uk
ALL THE FAVOURITES FROM THE TV CHANNEL

ORIGIN UK/US	Features all the characters, news, events and games
SPEED ✓✓	from the world of Toons. Hop into Sylvester and
INFO ✓✓✓✓	Tweety's mystery machine or visit Scooby Do. While
EASE ✓✓✓✓	the graphics and sound effects are good, it can be slow.

www.nickjr.com
THE NICKELODEON CHANNEL

ORIGIN US	Ideal for under 8s, this has a good selection of
SPEED ✓✓✓	games and quizzes to play either with an adult or
INFO ✓✓✓	solo. The major characters get a feature each and
VALUE ✓✓	you can personalise the site. The Red Rocket Store
EASE ✓✓✓✓	has an excellent selection of merchandise, but
	beware of shipping costs.

www.sesamestreet.com
THE CHILDREN'S TELEVISION WORKSHOP

ORIGIN US	Split into five sections: Let Ernie show you
SPEED ✓✓✓	Preschool Playground, get tips from the Parents
INFO ✓✓✓✓	Toolbox, learn about history in Kids City, give your
VALUE ✓✓✓	baby a workout in the Baby Workshop and meet the
EASE ✓✓✓✓	characters in Sesame Street Central. It's fun in parts,
	but quite worthy in tone. Another site dedicated to
	the very young is **www.funschool.com**.

www.yucky.com
THE YUCKIEST SITE ON THE INTERNET

ORIGIN US	Find out how to turn milk into slime or how much
SPEED ✓✓✓✓	you know about worms, yucky lives up to its name.
INFO ✓✓✓✓✓	Essentially this is an excellent, fun site that helps
EASE ✓✓✓✓	kids learn science and biology. There are guides for
	parents on how to get the best out of the site and
	links to recommended sites.

www.switcheroozoo.com
MAKE NEW ANIMALS

ORIGIN US	Over 6500 combinations of animals can be made at
SPEED ✓✓	this very entertaining web site, unfortunately, you
INFO ✓✓✓	need patience, Shockwave and a decent PC for it to
EASE ✓✓✓	work effectively.

www.bbc.co.uk/cbbc
CHILDREN'S BBC

ORIGIN UK
SPEED ✓✓✓
INFO ✓✓✓✓
EASE ✓✓✓✓

Built around *Blue Peter*, *Live & Kicking* and *Newsround*, you can catch up on the latest news, play games and find out about the stars of the programs. The web guide links to other recommended children's sites.

www.disney.com
WHERE THE MAGIC LIVES

ORIGIN US
SPEED ✓✓
INFO ✓✓✓✓
EASE ✓✓✓✓

Or more precisely where advertising lives, this site has an awful lot of adverts. It also has details on every aspect of the world of Disney, with some audio and video clips. In between the ads for other sites there are games, stories and competitions, but the whole thing is very slow. The British version www.disney.co.uk has much less advertising with most of the goodies.

www.ajkids.com
ASK JEEVES FOR KIDS

ORIGIN US
SPEED ✓✓✓
INFO ✓✓✓✓✓
EASE ✓✓✓

A search engine aimed at children, it's safe to use and is excellent for homework enquiries and games.

www.chickclick.com
FOR THE INDEPENDENT GIRL

ORIGIN US
SPEED ✓✓✓
INFO ✓✓✓✓
EASE ✓✓✓✓✓

What more could a girl want? Information on every key thing in life, what's cool, what's not, who's in who's not and most importantly who does Ben Affleck share breakfast with? You can set it up as your home page, with your own chickclick.com e-mail address and enter into the spirit by visiting the chat rooms. There are great links to sister sites too.

Classified Ads

see Auctions

Clip Art

see Art

Clothes

see Fashion

Clothes for Sport

see Sport

Competitions

www.loquax.co.uk
THE UK'S COMPETITION PORTAL

ORIGIN UK
SPEED ✓✓✓✓
INFO ✓✓✓✓✓
EASE ✓✓✓✓

This site doesn't give away prizes but lists the web sites that do. There are hundreds of competitions featured and, if you own a web site, they'll even run a competition for you. There are daily updates and special features such as "Pick of the Prizes" which features the best competitions the web has to offer with links to the relevant sites. For more competitions see **www.webcomp.co.uk** and **www.competitions-online.co.uk**.

Computers

It's no surprise that the number one place to buy a computer is over the internet. With these sites you won't go far wrong.

www.itreviews.co.uk
START HERE TO FIND THE BEST

ORIGIN UK	IT Reviews gives unbiased reports, not only on
SPEED ✓✓✓✓	computer products, but also software, games and
INFO ✓✓✓✓✓	books too. The site has a good search facility and a
EASE ✓✓✓✓	quick visit may save you loads of hassle when you

come to buy. For other excellent information sites try **www.zdnet.co.uk** or **www.cnet.com**, both have links to good on-line stores.

www.pricewatch.co.uk
START HERE FOR COMPUTER PRICES

ORIGIN UK	Pricewatch compares the prices of thousands of
SPEED ✓✓✓✓	computer hardware and software products. It's
INFO ✓✓✓✓	very good if you know what you're looking for, less
VALUE ✓✓✓✓✓	easy if not, so it pays to do some research first. It
EASE ✓✓✓	automatically puts you through to the store once

you've made your selection.

www.simply.co.uk
SIMPLY DOES IT

ORIGIN UK	An award-winning site and company that offers
SPEED ✓✓✓✓	a wide range of PCs and related products.
INFO ✓✓✓✓	Their strengths are speed, quality of service and
VALUE ✓✓✓✓	competitive prices. They also sell mobile phones.
EASE ✓✓✓✓	

www.tiny.com
LATEST TECHNOLOGY AT UNBEATABLE PRICES

ORIGIN UK
SPEED ✓✓✓✓
INFO ✓✓✓✓
VALUE ✓✓✓
EASE ✓✓✓✓

A businesslike site that includes all the details you'd need on their range of computers and peripherals for home and office use. Tiny are the UK's largest computer manufacturer and have a history of reliability and good deals. Shipping costs vary according to what you buy and where you live.

Other PC manufacturers site addresses:
Apple – www.apple.com
Dan – www.dan.co.uk
Dell – www.dell.co.uk
Elonex – www.elonex.co.uk
Evesham – www.evesham.com
Gateway – www.gateway.com/uk
Hewlett Packard – www.hp.com/uk
Time – www.timecomputers.com
Viglen – www.viglen.co.uk

Cosmetics

see Fashion

Days Out

see Travel

Dieting
see Health and Food & Drink

Do-it-yourself

*The web doesn't seem a natural home for do-it-yourself, but
there are some really useful sites and some great offers on equipment, especially furniture.*

Superstores

www.bandq.co.uk or www.diy.co.uk
THE DIY SUPERSTORES

ORIGIN UK	B&Q has an attractive site with lots of advice, tips
SPEED ✓✓✓	and information on projects for the home and
INFO ✓✓✓✓	garden, it also has an excellent searchable product
EASE ✓✓✓✓	database. You can't buy anything from it though. It's

the same at **www.homebase.co.uk**, which is also an
attractive site that tells you everything you need to
know about Homebase and their affordable products. Similarly from Jewson at **www.jewson.co.uk**,
although they do offer a hotline number and a
promise an on-line ordering system soon. The
Jewson site does have good links to DIY specialist
sites.

www.mfi.co.uk
MFI HOMEWORKS

ORIGIN UK	MFI offer a wide range of surprisingly good furni-
SPEED ✓✓✓	ture for home and office available for order on-line
INFO ✓✓✓✓	or via a hotline. Delivery is free.
VALUE ✓✓✓	
EASE ✓✓✓✓	

www.habitat.net
DESIGN OVER CONTENT

ORIGIN UK
SPEED ✓✓✓
INFO ✓✓✓
EASE ✓✓✓

A clever if slightly irritating web site giving an overview of what Habitat are about and what they stock, you can't order on-line though.

www.mccord.uk.com
McCORD'S CATALOGUE

ORIGIN UK
SPEED ✓✓✓
INFO ✓✓✓✓✓
EASE ✓✓✓

McCord's offer a huge range of furniture and accessories for the home via their on-line catalogue. It's very quick, easy-to-use, good value and delivery is £2.95 per order. Straight forward returns policy.

www.furniture-on-line.co.uk
SMART PLACE TO BUY FURNITURE

ORIGIN UK
SPEED ✓✓✓✓
INFO ✓✓✓✓
VALUE ✓✓✓✓
EASE ✓✓✓✓

This company has a nice web site offering a good range of furniture, many offers and free delivery. Shows 3-D views of some of the items.

DIY & home

www.screwfix.com
PRODUCTS FOR ALL DIY NEEDS

ORIGIN US
SPEED ✓✓✓
VALUE ✓✓✓✓✓✓
INFO ✓✓✓✓
EASE ✓✓✓

Screwfix offer excellent value for money with free delivery and wholesale prices on a massive range of DIY products. If only all on-line shops were like this.

www.cooksons.com

WHATEVER TOOLS YOU'RE AFTER THEY WILL BE HERE

ORIGIN US
SPEED ✓✓✓
INFO ✓✓✓✓
VALUE ✓✓✓✓
EASE ✓✓✓

Over 50,000 tools are available here, with free delivery on orders over £45. There are plenty of special offers and a loyalty scheme for regulars. W?WT

www.chiasmus.co.uk

FRESH AND FUNKY PRODUCTS FOR THE HOME

ORIGIN UK
SPEED ✓✓✓
INFO ✓✓✓✓✓
EASE ✓✓✓

Cute looking site with plenty of trendy products, especially good if you're looking for something a bit different. Free delivery on orders over £30.

www.bathroomexpress.co.uk

BETTER BATHROOMS

ORIGIN UK
SPEED ✓✓✓
INFO ✓✓
VALUE ✓✓✓✓
EASE ✓✓✓✓

A wide range of bathrooms and accessories are available at decent prices, with some interesting luxury items such as après-shower driers and some unique toilet seats. Delivery is based on how much you spend.

www.fmb.org.uk/consumers

THE FEDERATION OF MASTER BUILDERS

ORIGIN UK
SPEED ✓✓✓
INFO ✓✓✓✓✓
EASE ✓✓✓

How to avoid the cowboys and get the best out of a builder. There's information and articles on most aspects of home maintenance, plus hints on finding reputable help.

www.improveline.com
FIND A CONTRACTOR AND IDEAS

ORIGIN UK
SPEED ✓✓✓✓
INFO ✓✓✓✓
EASE ✓✓✓✓

Well-designed site offering information and inspiration for home improvements, there's also a service that puts you in touch with someone to do small jobs on the house within the hour. Inspiration comes in the form of thousands of categorised pictures, which are easily pulled up via a good search facility.

www.hometips.com
EXPERT ADVICE FOR YOUR HOME

ORIGIN US
SPEED ✓✓✓
INFO ✓✓✓✓
EASE ✓✓✓

American the advice may be but there is plenty for every homeowner. Split into six sections: there is a buying guide, advice on home care, DIY help, a tip sheet with reviews of other sites and books, a guide to how your house works and lastly dang good ideas. For a similar but less entertaining site try www.naturalhandyman.com or alternatively there is http://homedoctor.net/main.html which is very detailed.

www.diyfixit.co.uk
ON-LINE DIY ENCYCLOPAEDIA

ORIGIN UK
SPEED ✓✓✓
INFO ✓✓✓✓
EASE ✓✓✓

Get help with most DIY jobs using the search engine or browse by room or job type. The information is good but some guidance would help.

www.hi-revolution.com
HOME IMPROVEMENT WITHOUT HASSLE

ORIGIN UK	A nice idea, this is a service that matches your job
SPEED ✓✓✓	requirement to the right trade professional. It also
INFO ✓✓✓✓	assesses your chosen company on how well you
EASE ✓✓✓✓	think they performed the job.

www.thedesignstudio.com
GET THE RIGHT DESIGN

ORIGIN UK	This is an excellent database of wallpaper and fabric
SPEED ✓✓	samples, which is easy-to-use and good fun. Once
INFO ✓✓✓✓	you've selected your swatch you can then find the
EASE ✓✓✓	nearest supplier. You need some patience as it can be
	quite slow.

www.design-online.co.uk
NEED A DESIGNER?

ORIGIN UK	Design Online's mission is to put buyers and
SPEED ✓✓✓	suppliers in touch with each other and to use
INFO ✓✓✓✓✓	the internet to promote the use of well-designed
EASE ✓✓✓	products and services. You just search for the
	service you want and a list of suitable suppliers
	with contact details quickly appears.

www.bluedeco.com
BRITISH DESIGNERS ON-LINE

ORIGIN UK	This site offers a superb selection of designer prod-
SPEED ✓✓✓	ucts for the home, from furniture to ceramics, with
INFO ✓✓✓✓	free delivery to the UK. See also
VALUE ✓✓✓	**www.maelstrom.co.uk** W?WT who offer a similar
EASE ✓✓✓	range plus free delivery.

www.homesbydesign.co.uk

WHATEVER YOUR NEEDS

ORIGIN UK
SPEED ✓✓✓
INFO ✓✓✓✓✓
EASE ✓✓✓✓

Excellent magazine-style site with great advice on most DIY and home projects, they have regional listings of specialist suppliers and stores as well as features such as celebrity spots and ask a designer. You have to register to get the best out of it.

www.bhglive.com

BETTER HOMES AND GARDENS

ORIGIN US
SPEED ✓✓✓
INFO ✓✓✓✓✓
EASE ✓✓✓

There's more to this than DIY, but superb graphics and videos give this site the edge. It's American, so some information isn't applicable to the UK. The Home Encyclopaedia is excellent.

www.theplumber.com/hillsplb.html

AN ON-LINE PLUMBING CARE AND REPAIR KIT

ORIGIN US
SPEED ✓✓✓
INFO ✓✓✓✓
EASE ✓✓✓

Helps you fix all those niggly plumbing problems you'd normally call the real plumber out for. Even though it's American, much of the advice applies here. You can even learn about the history of plumbing. For bargains on plumbing gear go to www.plumbworld.co.uk.

www.architect-net.co.uk

ARCHITECTS AND BUILDING CONTRACTORS DIRECTORY

ORIGIN UK
SPEED ✓✓✓
INFO ✓✓✓
EASE ✓✓✓

Find an architect to design your next home, using the regional directory. Not a great site, but useful for good links to related sites.

Doctors

see Health

Drink

see Food & Drink

Education

www.bbc.co.uk/education

GET EQUIPPED FOR LIFE

ORIGIN UK
SPEED ✓✓✓✓
INFO ✓✓✓✓
EASE ✓✓✓✓

A superb learning resource, whether you are 3 or 33, with information on their education-related programs and activities. However, it can be limiting as each section tends to be tied to a particular program. There are also sections in French, Italian, German and Spanish.

www.eduweb.co.uk

THE INTERNET SERVICE FOR TEACHERS AND PUPILS

ORIGIN UK
SPEED ✓✓✓✓
INFO ✓✓✓✓✓
EASE ✓✓✓✓

In subscribing to EduWeb you are getting access to:
1. A massive amount of data for use on homework.
2. Advice on how to study and use the curriculum.
3. A net pen pals service for children and teenagers.
4. Advice for teachers on projects.
5. Resources for teachers and a discussion forum.
6. Where to find the best school.
For a similar U.S. site, go to www.edview.com, which has a huge listing of sites approved by teachers.

www.schoolzone.co.uk

UK'S TOP EDUCATIONAL SEARCH ENGINE

ORIGIN UK
SPEED ✓✓✓✓
INFO ✓✓✓✓✓
EASE ✓✓✓✓

Access to over 30,000 sites and resources, all checked by teachers, schoolzone is very comprehensive. Everything recommended is rated according to how useful it is. There is free software to download, plus homework help, career advice, teacher support and much more.

www.virtualschool.co.uk
COURSES DELIVERED TO YOUR PC

ORIGIN UK
SPEED ✓✓✓✓
INFO ✓✓✓✓
VALUE ✓✓✓
EASE ✓✓✓✓

Designed to allow you to learn from home, you can get courses on English, Maths, Science, History, Geography, Religion, French, Italian, Russian, Psychology and Sociology. Cost is around £60, and they are approved and recommended by many authorities. They can also offer help with revision and there are experts on-line at certain times.

www.ngfl.gov.uk
THE NATIONAL GRID FOR LEARNING

ORIGIN UK
SPEED ✓✓✓✓
INFO ✓✓✓✓
EASE ✓✓✓✓

The official government education site, it has sections for every aspect of learning. There is information for everyone, whatever their educational needs, along with details on the key museums, galleries and libraries. There is also a section on education in the Commonwealth. For information on the National Curriculum see **www.qca.org.uk**. For information on the Scottish education system see **www.sqa.org.uk**.

www.dfee.gov.uk/nc
NATIONAL CURRICULUM REVEALED

ORIGIN UK
SPEED ✓✓✓
INFO ✓✓✓✓✓
EASE ✓✓✓✓

Very detailed explanation of the National Curriculum and desired pupil outcomes.

www.hobsons.co.uk
GLOBAL CAREERS AND EDUCATION ADVICE

ORIGIN UK/US
SPEED ✓✓✓
INFO ✓✓✓✓✓
EASE ✓✓✓✓

Hobsons' aim is to provide students, advisers, parents, carers and professionals with information on courses and careers. Its has an established reputation for finding jobs for university leavers, but is excellent for young people who need career advice. Also see www.oncourse.co.uk, which has a London oriented view.

www.datalake.com
THE LIVE LEARNING RESOURCE

ORIGIN UK
SPEED ✓✓✓
INFO ✓✓✓✓
EASE ✓✓✓✓

Datalake aims to enable you to find the right course, and eventually the right job too. It's all cleverly tied together and, although it is geared to IT, local government, engineering and medicine, all students will find it useful. It also carries information on schools and local government departments.

www.edunet.com
THE DIGITAL EDUCATION NETWORK

ORIGIN UK
SPEED ✓✓✓✓
INFO ✓✓✓✓
EASE ✓✓✓✓

The D.E.N. will help you find the right course and give information on what resources are available to help. They offer a worldwide service, hosting forums and discussion groups, giving awards for good education sites. They are very strong on English as a foreign language.

www.open.ac.uk
THE OPEN UNIVERSITY

ORIGIN UK
SPEED ✓✓✓✓
INFO ✓✓✓
EASE ✓✓✓✓

This is the world's leader in distance education. Learn about the courses and find out what the OU can do for you. All it needs is a good set of links to related sites.

www.gcse.com
GCSE ANSWERS

ORIGIN UK
SPEED ✓✓✓✓
INFO ✓✓✓✓
EASE ✓✓✓

This is a developing site that has tests and past papers for GCSE exams on English and Maths. It is building fast with much available on other exams, including tips on how to get good results and information on the various examining bodies.

www.a-levels.co.uk
PASS THAT EXAM

ORIGIN UK
SPEED ✓✓✓
INFO ✓✓✓✓✓
EASE ✓✓✓

This promises to be an excellent, well-targeted site, with plenty of detail on the key exams. However, it seems in danger of becoming a bit too commercial, with corporate intervention and hoo-ha about awards it's won. It hasn't been updated for some time.
For help with homework and other reference sites see page 155.

Electrical Goods and Appliances

www.comet.co.uk
ALWAYS LOW PRICES, GUARANTEED

ORIGIN UK
SPEED ✓✓✓
INFO ✓✓✓✓✓
VALUE ✓✓✓✓
EASE ✓✓✓✓

Lots of products, split into five key sections:
1. Kitchen, for washing machines, microwaves and cookers.
2. Household, with vacuums, irons and ionisers and air purifiers.
3. Entertainment, featuring TV, music, games and keyboards.
4. Computing and communication, offering PCs and mobiles.

5. Personal care, with hairdryers, shavers and dental products.

Finance deals abound and there's information on the products. Delivery costs vary.

www.dixons.co.uk
OFFERS GALORE

ORIGIN UK
SPEED ✓✓✓✓
INFO ✓✓✓
VALUE ✓✓✓✓
EASE ✓✓✓✓

The Dixons site has plenty of offers and reflects what you'd find in their stores very well. It has a similar but slightly wider product range to Comet, with an additional photographic section. Delivery is £3.25 an item.

www.priceright.co.uk
ONE STOP SHOP FOR ELECTRICAL APPLIANCES

ORIGIN UK
SPEED ✓✓✓✓
INFO ✓✓✓✓
VALUE ✓✓✓✓✓
EASE ✓✓✓✓

Priceright have a good reputation for value, and you can sense it straight away as the site unfolds. Free delivery on all products is the first thing you see, then the automatic 5% discount when you join. Their range is excellent, covering most of the major brands and product categories.

www.hed.co.uk
HOME ELECTRICAL DIRECT

ORIGIN UK
SPEED ✓✓✓
INFO ✓✓✓
VALUE ✓✓✓✓✓
EASE ✓✓✓✓

Their motto is "the lowest prices guaranteed all year round, and that's a promise". They have a very large range of goods covering all the key product categories minus cameras. Delivery is free. **W?WT**
See also another **W?WT** site **www.electricalappliancesdirect.co.uk**.

www.homeplus.co.uk
HOME SHOPPING MADE EASY

ORIGIN UK	A clear, straight forward site that has a wide range
SPEED ✓✓✓	of appliances for the home, DIY products, pets and
INFO ✓✓✓	car accessories. They only deliver to the UK main-
VALUE ✓✓✓✓	land, but it's free.
EASE ✓✓✓✓	

www.richersounds.com
A PROMISE TO BEAT EVERY OTHER WEBSITE BY £50

ORIGIN UK	Bargain hunters will want to include this site on
SPEED ✓✓✓	their list. Similar to the other electrical goods
INFO ✓✓	retailers but with a leaning towards music and TVs,
VALUE ✓✓✓✓	with plenty of offers. However, there was no search
EASE ✓✓✓✓	facility at the time of going to print, and delivery
	isn't free.

www.appliancespares.co.uk
FIX IT YOURSELF

ORIGIN UK	Ezee-Fix has thousands of spare parts for a massive
SPEED ✓✓✓✓	range of products including fridges, cookers,
INFO ✓✓	microwaves, vacuum cleaners, etc. All it needs is on-
VALUE ✓✓✓	line instructions, and more details on the products
EASE ✓✓✓✓	and it would be perfect.

www.bull-electrical.com
FOR THE SPECIALIST

ORIGIN UK	Fascinating to visit, this site offers every sort of
SPEED ✓✓✓✓	electronic device, from divining rods, to radio kits and
INFO ✓✓✓✓	spy cameras. There are four basic sections:
VALUE ✓✓✓✓	1. Surplus electronic, scientific and optical goods –
EASE ✓✓✓	even steam engines.

2. Links to specialist shops such as spy equipment
   and hydroponics.

3. Free services such as auctions and even a joke shop!
4. Web services, shopping cart technology for example.

For computers also see page 40.

Electricity

see Utilities

Employment

see Jobs

Encyclopaedia

see Reference

Estate Agents

see Property

Fashion, Clothes and Beauty Products

Selling fashion and designer gear is another net success, as customers flock to the great discounts that are on offer. The big brands have never been cheaper, although many people still prefer to actually try on clothes in a shop. However, the good sites all offer a convenient returns policy.

www.vogue.co.uk
THE LATEST NEWS FROM BRITISH VOGUE

ORIGIN UK
SPEED ✓✓✓✓
INFO ✓✓✓✓
EASE ✓✓✓✓

An absolute must for the serious follower of fashion. There's the latest catwalk news and views, and a handy who's who of fashion. There's also a section on jobs, and you can order a subscription too. For a similar experience try www.ellemag.com or the slightly less fashion oriented but more fun www.cosmomag.com.

www.designersdirect.com
THE BIG BRANDS AT HUGE DISCOUNTS

ORIGIN US
SPEED ✓✓✓✓
INFO ✓✓✓✓
VALUE ✓✓✓✓
EASE ✓✓✓✓

If you are into designer brands, then this excellent site may be all you'll ever need. Split into four major sections: men's, women's, eyewear and footwear, each is clearly laid out with good quality, large photos of each item. The range is good, as are the prices. Delivery charges vary according to what you spend. Also try www.designerheaven.co.uk who offer free worldwide delivery.

www.intofashion.com
GET INTO FASHION

ORIGIN UK
SPEED ✓✓✓✓
INFO ✓✓✓✓
VALUE ✓✓✓✓
EASE ✓✓✓✓

With sections on jewellery, hair accessories, scarves, bags and, of course, clothes, Intofashion offers a complete service, backed by excellent design and picture quality. You can search the site by designer or by product or browse the best buys. Delivery is free in the UK. For another similar site try www.theclothesstore.com who also have a good selection of clothes and accessories, but charge for delivery to the UK.

www.zercon.com
CUT-PRICE DESIGNER CLOTHES FOR MEN AND WOMEN

ORIGIN UK
SPEED ✓✓✓✓
INFO ✓✓✓✓
VALUE ✓✓✓✓
EASE ✓✓✓✓

Not a big range of clothes but excellent prices. Clear, no nonsense design, makes the site easy-to-use and they are members of the Which? Web trader scheme so shopping is secure. W?WT

www.apc.fr
FRENCH CHIC FROM A.P.C.

ORIGIN FRANCE
SPEED ✓✓✓✓
INFO ✓✓✓
VALUE ✓✓
EASE ✓✓✓✓

Unusual in style and for something a little different A.P.C.'s site is worth a visit. Delivery is expensive, in line with the clothes, which are beautifully designed and well presented.

www.diesel.co.uk
COOL DESIGN

ORIGIN UK
SPEED ✓✓✓✓
INFO ✓✓✓
VALUE ✓✓✓
EASE ✓✓✓✓

Interesting design and a good choice of contemporary clothing from Diesel for both men and women. Delivery is £4 per order.

www.shoe-shop.com
FOR FABULOUS FOOTWARE

ORIGIN UK
SPEED ✓✓✓
INFO ✓✓✓✓
VALUE ✓✓✓✓
EASE ✓✓✓✓

This site is the ultimate shoe shop with shoes for all occasions. The site is well designed and easy to use, what's more, delivery is free in the UK.

www.gap.com
FOR US RESIDENTS ONLY

ORIGIN US	A clear, uncluttered design makes shopping here
SPEED ✓✓✓	easy if you live in the United States! For UK
INFO ✓✓✓✓	residents it's window-shopping only.
VALUE ✓✓✓	
EASE ✓✓✓✓	

www.next.co.uk
THE NEXT DIRECTORY

ORIGIN UK	The on-line version of the Next catalogue is available,
SPEED ✓✓✓	including clothes for men, women and children as well
INFO ✓✓✓✓	as products for the home. Prices are the same as the
VALUE ✓✓✓	directory, delivery is charged according to spend but
EASE ✓✓✓✓	return of unwanted goods is free.

www.dressmart.com
FOR MEN

ORIGIN UK	With all the key designers represented, a wide range,
SPEED ✓✓✓✓	competitive prices and free delivery, what more
INFO ✓✓✓✓	could the best dressed of men want? It's quick, easy-
VALUE ✓✓✓✓	to-use, with good quality pictures.
EASE ✓✓✓✓	

The Arcadia Group

www.arcadia.co.uk
THE UK'S LEADING FASHION RETAILER

ORIGIN UK	www.su214.co.uk – men's fashion
SPEED ✓✓✓	www.racinggreen.co.uk – fashion
INFO ✓✓✓✓	www.dorothyperkins.co.uk – women's clothes
VALUE ✓✓✓✓	www.tops.co.uk – young women's fashion at Topshop
EASE ✓✓✓✓	www.topman.co.uk – men's clothes
	www.burtonmenswear.co.uk – men's clothes

www.hawkshead.com – outdoor clothes
www.principles.co.uk – for both men and women
www.zoom.co.uk – fashion
www.evans.co.uk – for mature women
The Arcadia Group has over 1200 stores in the UK, and the web sites are accessible, easy-to-use and offer good value for money. Each has its own personality that reflects the real life store. Delivery charges vary.

www.fashionbot.com

THE FASHION SEARCH ENGINE

ORIGIN UK	Quickly search the major on-line stores (mainly
SPEED ✓✓✓✓	those from the Arcadia Group) and compare prices.
INFO ✓✓✓✓	Just click on the item you want to check. If you
VALUE ✓✓✓✓	can't find what you want here try www.fashion.net,
EASE ✓✓✓✓	an American site that also offers news, jobs and a
	good set of links to other fashion sites.

General clothes stores

www.kaysnet.com

KAYS CATALOGUE

ORIGIN UK	Massive range combined with value for money is the
SPEED ✓✓✓✓	formula for success with Kays. While they lead with
INFO ✓✓✓✓	clothes, there are plenty of other sections outside
VALUE ✓✓✓✓	of that: jewellery, home entertainment, toys, etc.
EASE ✓✓✓✓	Delivery charge depends on how much you spend.

www.freemans.co.uk
FREE DELIVERY IN THE UK AND GOOD PRICES

ORIGIN UK
SPEED ✓✓✓
INFO ✓✓✓✓
VALUE ✓✓✓✓
EASE ✓✓✓✓

Not the full catalogue but there's loads to choose from including top brands. It's split into four sections – men, women, children and sports. See also **www.shoppersuniverse.com** for the Great Universal stores catalogue.

www.thebestofbritish.com
GREAT FOR THE TRADITIONAL AND THE NEW

ORIGIN UK
SPEED ✓✓✓
INFO ✓✓✓✓
VALUE ✓✓✓✓
EASE ✓✓✓✓

Owned by the *Daily Telegraph*, all the brands are here, covering a wide variety of goods, but mainly clothes and accessories. Search the site by designer, brand or product type. Delivery is charged although check as occasionally it's free.

Specialist clothes stores

www.bloomingmarvellous.co.uk
MATERNITY WEAR

ORIGIN UK
SPEED ✓✓✓✓
INFO ✓✓✓✓
VALUE ✓✓✓✓
EASE ✓✓✓✓

The UK's leading store in maternity and babywear has an attractive site that features a good selection of clothes and nursery products. There are no discounts on the clothes, but they do have regular sales with some good bargains. Delivery in the UK is £3.95 per order.

www.noveltytogs.com
FOR CHARACTER MERCHANDISE

ORIGIN UK
SPEED ✓✓✓✓
INFO ✓✓✓✓
VALUE ✓✓✓
EASE ✓✓✓✓

Merchandise for *The Simpsons*, *South Park*, *Garfield* and *Peanuts*. There are the usual T-shirts plus boxer shorts, socks and nightshirts. Delivery is free for the UK and there are links to other character web sites. **W?WT**

www.tienet.co.uk
THE INTERNET TIE STORE

ORIGIN UK	Hundreds of ties in seemingly every colour and
SPEED ✓✓✓✓	design, there are sections on fashion ties, bowties,
INFO ✓✓✓✓	tartan and character ties. Selection and payment is
VALUE ✓✓✓✓	simple, but some of the pictures are quite blurred
EASE ✓✓✓✓	and the patterns are sometimes difficult to see.
	Delivery charge depends on size of order.

Underwear and lingerie

www.smartbras.com
BRAS, BASQUES AND BRIEFS

ORIGIN UK	The easy, embarrassment free way to buy
SPEED ✓✓✓✓	underwear. Choose from a selection of around 200
INFO ✓✓✓✓	lingerie products including brand names at high
VALUE ✓✓✓	street prices. Delivery is £2.50 for the UK.
EASE ✓✓✓✓	

For up-market lingerie try **www.rigbyandpeller.com**. *For value go to the excellent* **www.easyshop.co.uk**. *For specialists in men's underwear try either* **www.kiniki.com** *or for "underwear with pulling power"* **www.shortsite.com**.

Accessories and jewellery

www.jewellers.net
THE BIGGEST RANGE ON THE NET

ORIGIN UK	Excellent range of products, fashion jewellery, gifts,
SPEED ✓✓✓✓	gold and silver and the watch section is particularly
INFO ✓✓✓✓	strong. There is also information on the history of
VALUE ✓✓✓✓	gems, the manufacturers and brands available.
EASE ✓✓✓✓	Delivery to the UK is free, and there is a 30-day no
	quibble returns policy. W?WT

www.hpj.co.uk
HALF PRICE JEWELLERS

ORIGIN UK	The UK's leading discount jeweller offers a cheap,
SPEED ✓✓✓	reliable service with delivery being £2.95 per order,
INFO ✓✓✓✓	with next day service at £4.95. Excellent prices
VALUE ✓✓✓✓	compared to the high street.
EASE ✓✓✓✓	

www.topbrands.net
WATCH HEAVEN

ORIGIN UK	A large range of watches including Swatch, Casio, G
SPEED ✓✓✓✓	Shock, Baby G and Seiko are available here. The site
INFO ✓✓✓✓	is fast and easy-to-use, but a better search facility
VALUE ✓✓✓	would save time. Delivery is free for the UK, but
EASE ✓✓✓✓	prices appear to be similar to the high street.

Cosmetics

www.bodyshop.co.uk
ISSUES, SELF-ESTEEM AND COSMETICS

ORIGIN UK	Balancing the rights of the under-privileged with the
SPEED ✓✓✓	demands of a commercial cosmetics company. There
INFO ✓✓✓✓✓	is good product information but you can't buy on-
EASE ✓✓✓✓	line. However, download and play with the virtual
	makeover.

www.fragrancenet.com
WORLD'S LARGEST DISCOUNT FRAGRANCE STORE

ORIGIN US	A massive range of perfumes for men and women,
SPEED ✓✓✓✓	every brand is represented and there are some excel-
INFO ✓✓✓✓	lent offers. However the site is American with ship-
VALUE ✓✓✓	ping costs of up to $23 dollars for 5 items or more.
EASE ✓✓✓✓	

www.directcosmetics.com
WIDE RANGE AND THE BEST PRICES

ORIGIN UK
SPEED ✓✓✓✓
INFO ✓✓✓✓
VALUE ✓✓✓✓
EASE ✓✓✓✓

They claim to offer a wide range of perfumes with up to 90% off UK recommended retail prices plus the latest news from the big brand names. The site is quick and easy-to-use and the offers are genuine; however, there is a delivery charge. See also www.perfumeshopping.com who offer 1000 perfumes and fragrances, and Smellsearch, a facility which matches a perfume to the smells you stipulate.

Films

see Movies

Flowers

www.interflora.co.uk
TURNING THOUGHTS INTO FLOWERS

ORIGIN UK
SPEED ✓✓✓✓
INFO ✓✓✓✓
VALUE ✓✓✓
EASE ✓✓✓✓

Interflora can send flowers to over 140 countries, many on the same day as the order. They'll have a selection to send for virtually every occasion, and they even offer a reminder service. The service is excellent, although they are not very up front on delivery costs, which can be high. If you can't get what you need here then try www.teleflorist.co.uk who offer a similar service. For a wider selection and a more international service go to www.freeflowers.com.

www.clareflorist.co.uk
STYLISH BOUQUETS AND PRETTY PICTURES

You know what you're sending as all the bouquets

ORIGIN UK
SPEED ✓✓✓
INFO ✓✓✓✓
VALUE ✓✓✓✓
EASE ✓✓✓✓

are photographed. Easy-to-use with three price rates, good customer service and delivery to UK at £2.35.

Finance, Banking and Shares

The internet is proving to be a real winner when it comes to personal finance, product comparison and home share dealing. With these sites you will get the latest advice and may even make some money.

General finance sites and mortgages

www.fsa.gov.uk
FINANCIAL SERVICES AUTHORITY

ORIGIN UK
SPEED ✓✓✓
INFO ✓✓✓✓
EASE ✓✓✓✓

The regulating body that you can go to if you need help with your rights or if you want to find out about financial products; it will also help you to verify that the financial institution you're dealing with is legitimate.

www.find.co.uk
INTERNET DIRECTORY FOR FINANCIAL SERVICES

ORIGIN UK
SPEED ✓✓✓✓
INFO ✓✓✓✓✓
EASE ✓✓✓✓

Hundreds of links split into eight sections: investing, insurance, information, share dealing, banking and saving, mortgages and loans, business services and a centre for Independent Financial Advisers.

www.ft.com
www.ftyourmoney.com
FINANCIAL TIMES

ORIGIN UK	FT.com offers up-to-date news and information.
SPEED ✓✓✓	Your Money section is biased towards personal
INFO ✓✓✓✓	finance, is easy-to-use and provides sound, indepen-
EASE ✓✓✓✓	dent advice for everyone.

www.moneyextra.com
www.moneyworld.co.uk
www.emfinance.com
THE UK'S PERSONAL FINANCE GUIDE

ORIGIN UK	Combined, these sister sites probably make up the
SPEED ✓✓✓	most comprehensive personal finance information
INFO ✓✓✓✓✓	available.
EASE ✓✓✓✓	

Moneyextra concentrates on comparison tables for mortgages, loans and other financial services.

MoneyWorld is biased towards personal finance with added advice for investors; it also has an excellent financial glossary as well as tax and mortgage calculators.

Emfinance claim to be the UK's first on-line mortgage broker with support from several leading lenders.

www.fool.co.uk
THE MOTLEY FOOL

ORIGIN US	Finance with a sense of fun, The Fool is exciting and
SPEED ✓✓✓	a real education in shrewdness. It not only takes the
INFO ✓✓✓✓	mystery out of share dealing but gives great advice
EASE ✓✓✓✓	on investment and personal finance. You need to
	register to get the best out of it.

www.thisismoney.com
MONEY NEWS AND ADVICE

ORIGIN UK

SPEED ✓✓✓✓

INFO ✓✓✓✓✓

EASE ✓✓✓✓

Easy-to-use, reliable, 24-hour financial advice from the Daily Mail group. It has loads of information on all aspects of personal finance and is particularly good for comparison tools, especially mortgages.

www.blays.co.uk
BLAYS GUIDES

ORIGIN UK

SPEED ✓✓✓✓

INFO ✓✓✓✓✓

EASE ✓✓✓✓

Excellent design and impartial advice make the Blays guide a must visit site for personal finance. It has all the usual suspects: mortgages, savings, etc., plus very good sections for students. Look at the "which is best value" for phone service and utilities.

www.moneynet.co.uk
IMPARTIAL AND COMPREHENSIVE

ORIGIN UK

SPEED ✓✓✓

INFO ✓✓✓✓

EASE ✓✓✓✓

Rated as one of the best independent personal finance sites, it covers over 100 mortgage lenders, has a user-friendly search facility plus help with conveyancing and financial calculators.

For similar straight forward sites with comprehensive information try:

www.iii.co.uk – Interactive investor international is a good, jargon-free site.

www.sort.co.uk – Good design and advice backed by personal help. You can also get financial health checks for a fee.

www.thedeal.net – A high tech "financial lifestyle" magazine, there are some good deals if you're patient, as well as interesting sections on the home, travel and entertainment.

Mortgage specialists

www.charcoalonline.co.uk
INDEPENDENT ADVICE

ORIGIN UK
SPEED ✓✓✓
INFO ✓✓✓✓
EASE ✓✓✓✓

This established independent adviser offers information on over 400 mortgages from over 45 lenders. There are also sections on pensions, investments and insurance. For other independent advice try www.mortgages-online.co.uk. Alternatively, Your Mortgage magazine at www.yourmortgage.co.uk, presents the latest news and deals from their well designed and easy-to-use site.

It's worth shopping around so check out these sites too:

www.mortgagepoint.co.uk – Geared towards first time buyers.

www.mortgageman.u-net.com – Aimed at the self-employed or those having difficulty getting a mortgage from the usual lenders, or with CCJ's.

www.eloan.com/uk – Good general site offering mortgages from over 50 lenders.

Insurance

www.homequote.co.uk
INSURANCE QUOTES AT THE TOUCH OF A BUTTON

ORIGIN UK
SPEED ✓✓✓
INFO ✓✓✓✓
EASE ✓✓✓✓

Fill in your details and get free, no obligation quotes from several major companies for either contents or buildings insurance, or both. It's also worth shopping around so check out www.insurancewide.com and www.screentrade.co.uk who both cover other types of insurance too.

www.life-search.co.uk
LIFE ASSURANCE

ORIGIN	UK
SPEED	✓✓✓
INFO	✓✓✓✓✓
EASE	✓✓✓✓

A nicely designed site that takes you through the minefield that is the life assurance market. An excellent jargon buster that will provide quotes, but can't arrange policies on-line.

Investing and share dealing

www.shwab-worldwide.com/europe
CHARLES SHWAB EUROPE

ORIGIN	US
SPEED	✓✓✓
INFO	✓✓✓✓✓
EASE	✓✓✓✓

Although you'll need to register and put up a deposit, this is the biggest and probably the most reliable internet share dealer for the UK. You can trade on-line and get 30 days of free commission when you sign up.

Any of the following are worth checking out, they are all good sites, each with a slightly different focus, so find the one that suits you:

www.barclays-stockbrokers.co.uk – Good value for smaller share deals, 1% commission and a minimum of £11.99, possibly the best for beginners.

www.tdwaterhouse.co.uk – Slightly more expensive than Barclays, but still quite good value, well designed but could do with a glossary.

www.sharepeople.com – Independent, British and proud of it, nice design, easy-to-use with lots of explanation about what goes on. Flat fee of £17.50 on all trades.

www.thestreet.co.uk – Not a dealer but this site offers a great deal of up to the minute market information.

www.sharexpress.co.uk – The Halifax share dealing service that is a good beginner's site and charges competitively.

www.ukinvest.com – Part of the Freeserve
network, its strengths are in news and company
information.

www.itsonline.co.uk – Well-designed site that
concentrates on explaining and campaigning for
investment trusts.

Banks

www.bankfacts.org.uk
BRITISH BANKERS ASSOCIATION

ORIGIN UK
SPEED ✓✓✓✓
INFO ✓✓✓✓
EASE ✓✓✓✓

Answers to the most common questions about banking, advice about internet banks, the banking code and
general information, there's also a facility that helps
you resurrect dormant accounts.

Here are the high street and internet banks,
building societies and the on-line facilities they
currently offer:

www.abbeynational.co.uk – New web site with new
management service; however you can't register
on-line.

www.alliance-leicester.co.uk – A comprehensive
service offering mortgages, insurance and banking. The site is slow due to the large amount of
graphics involved.

www.bankofscotland.co.uk – Home and Office
Banking (HOBS) is an established system, which
allows for an efficient and wide ranging personal
banking service, however you need Shockwave to
get the best out of it.

www.barclays.co.uk – One of the original innova-
tors in internet banking, they offer an exhaustive
service covering all aspects of personal and small
business banking. It can be slow.

www.bradford-bingley.co.uk – Basic site showing information on the B&B and their services, internet banking is on the way.

www.citibank.co.uk – Very impressive site with a complete personal banking service with competitive rates. Citibank have few branches and this is their attempt at a bigger foothold in the UK.

www.co-operativebank.co.uk – Acknowledged as the most comprehensive of the banking sites and it's easy-to-use. Excellent, but they have also launched the trendier and more competitive Smile banking site **www.smile.co.uk**, which is aimed at a younger audience.

www.egg.co.uk – Low rates combined with an attempt at individuality make Egg a bank with a difference. You can also go shopping at 100 retailers via the site and get 2% cash back if you use your Egg card.

www.firstactive.co.uk – Irritating graphics can make a visit here a frustrating experience, that aside there is a wide range of personal finance services available including mortgages.

www.halifax.co.uk – Comprehensive range of services via an easy-to-use and well-designed site. You'll find a great deal of advice and information all clearly explained on the home site.

www.banking.hsbc.co.uk – Straight forward and easy-to-use site offering on-line banking alongside the usual services from HSBC. Like the Co-Op they've also launched a trendier internet bank called **www.firstdirect.co.uk**, which offers all the main site does from an impressive site.

www.lloydstsb.co.uk – Combined with Scottish Widows and the Post Office, Lloyds offer a more rounded and comprehensive financial service than most. The on-line banking is well established and efficient, and there is help for small businesses too.

www.nationwide.co.uk – Don't be put off by the dated appearance of the Nationwide site which looks rather like a tabloid newspaper, they offer a complete on-line banking service as well as loans and mortgages.

www.natwest.com – NatWest offer both on-line banking and share dealing, with good sections for students and small businesses, it's got a nice design, it's easy-to-use and there is a non-animated version as well.

www.woolwich.co.uk – On-line banking, car buying (**www.motorbase.co.uk**) and a WAP technology mobile phone banking service plus all the other usual personal financial services make the Woolwich site a little different.

www.virgin-direct.co.uk – Access to the Virgin One account, which you can manage via this site, there's also a share dealing service and a directory of other products too.

www.ybs.co.uk – No on-line service but you can get details of the Yorkshire Building Society's very competitive rates on mortgages and savings.

Tax

www.inlandrevenue.gov.uk
TALK TO THE TAXMAN

ORIGIN UK
SPEED ✓✓✓✓
INFO ✓✓✓✓
EASE ✓✓✓

The Inland Revenue has a very informative site where you can get help on all aspects of tax. There's a good set of links to other government departments and you can order extra forms via the site.

www.tax.org.uk
CHARTERED INSTITUTE OF TAXATION

ORIGIN UK
SPEED ✓✓✓
INFO ✓✓✓✓✓
EASE ✓✓✓

A great resource, they don't provide information on individual questions but they can put you in touch with a qualified adviser. It's a good place to start if you have a problem with your tax. For the latest tax news go to http://e-tax.org.uk, which is very comprehensive.

http://listen.to/taxman
UK PAYE TAX CALCULATOR

ORIGIN UK
SPEED ✓✓✓
INFO ✓✓✓✓
EASE ✓✓✓✓✓

Amazingly fast, just input your gross earnings and your tax and actual earnings are calculated.

Business

www.businesslink.co.uk
YOUR BUSINESS IS OUR BUSINESS

ORIGIN UK
SPEED ✓✓✓
INFO ✓✓✓✓✓
EASE ✓✓✓✓

UK oriented business advice and information site, with regional centres where you can get help with most business problems and development locally. If you want to change your business, here's a good place to start.

www.economist.com
THE ECONOMIST MAGAZINE

ORIGIN UK	The airport's best-selling magazine goes on-line with
SPEED ✓✓✓✓✓	a wide-ranging site that covers business and politics
INFO ✓✓✓✓✓	world-wide. You can get access to the archive and
EASE ✓✓✓✓	also their excellent country surveys. If you're in
	business, you need this in your favourites box.

www.asiannet.com
BUSINESS INFORMATION ON ASIA

ORIGIN US	Market information, news, services and links all
SPEED ✓✓✓	geared to the main Asian markets of which each has
INFO ✓✓✓✓	a feature site. There are company profiles as well as
EASE ✓✓✓	an on-line shop where you can contact companies to
	get product samples.

www.islamiq.com
ISLAMIC FINANCE AND BUSINESS

ORIGIN UK	Excellent British site aimed at being in their words
SPEED ✓✓✓✓	"a finance and investment portal synchronised with
INFO ✓✓✓✓✓	Islamic principles". There is a great deal of informa-
EASE ✓✓✓✓	tion about personal finance, share dealing and
	investing as well as news and shopping.

Miscellaneous

www.young-money.co.uk
ON-LINE MONEY GAME SHOW

ORIGIN UK	Combines general knowledge and financial games
SPEED ✓✓✓	aimed at turning the little ones into financial whizz-
INFO ✓✓✓✓	kids of the future. There's a lot that most adults
EASE ✓✓✓✓	can learn form the site as well as it's a fun way of
	learning about the world of finance. You need
	Shockwave for it to work.

www.uk.sage.com
BUSINESS SOFTWARE

ORIGIN UK	If you need accounting software to solve virtually
SPEED ✓✓✓	any sort of problem or provide a new service, you
INFO ✓✓✓✓✓	should find it here. Sage has a good reputation for
VALUE ✓✓✓	helping small businesses.
EASE ✓✓✓✓	

Finding Someone

Where to find a phone number, contacts for business and the home.

www.yell.co.uk
THE YELLOW PAGES ON-LINE – JUST YELL!

ORIGIN UK	Split into five key services:
SPEED ✓✓✓	
INFO ✓✓✓✓✓	
EASE ✓✓✓✓✓	

1. The search engine. This enables you to search for the business or service you want by region, type or name. It is very quick, and you get plenty of details on each entry.
2. Travel – which links you up with one of the biggest on-line travel agents **www.expedia.com**
3. Property – which links you to **www.homesight.co.uk** an advice site for moving house or for looking up the details of a region or town.
4. Shopping – a directory for on-line stores, covering mainstream merchandise.
5. Business – provides sections on international trading, UK business and a business-to-business direct marketing channel.

There is an equivalent service in the USA with the intriguing title of **www.bigfoot.com**. It is very similar to Yell, except there is a feature that enables you to search for people's, as well as business e-mail addresses.

www.scoot.co.uk
THE SIMPLE WAY TO FIND SOMEONE

ORIGIN UK
SPEED ✓✓✓
INFO ✓✓✓✓✓
EASE ✓✓✓✓✓

Register, type in the person's name, or profession, then hit the scoot button and your answer comes back in seconds.

www.thomweb.co.uk
THE ANSWER COMES OUT OF THE BLUE

ORIGIN UK
SPEED ✓✓
INFO ✓✓✓✓✓
EASE ✓✓✓✓

Thomson's local directories are available on-line. It's an impressive site but it's a shame it's so slow. It's divided up into six major categories:

1. Business finder – search using a combination of name, type of business or region. The results are less accurate then Yell; ask for a plumber in a town and you may get every plumber for miles around.
2. People finder – find out people's phone numbers and home or e-mail addresses.
3. Comprehensive local information is available on the major cities and regions.
4. 5-day weather forecasts.
5. Net Community with sections on chat sites, personal ads, news groups and on-line events.
6. Contact Thomson's or place ads.

www.phonenumbers.net
THE PHONE NUMBER OF VIRTUALLY EVERYONE WHO'S LISTED

ORIGIN US
SPEED ✓✓✓✓
INFO ✓✓✓
EASE ✓✓✓✓

Start by clicking on the country or area you need, then you can easily find the phone, fax or e-mail address of anyone who is in the book. It also has a section with a number of links to other search engines such as Yell.

www.bt.com
BRITISH TELECOM SERVICES

ORIGIN UK
SPEED ✓✓
INFO ✓✓✓✓
EASE ✓✓

BT offers a site that gives a very thorough overview of its services. To get the best out of it you need to register. Have your account number handy and you can view your telephone bill.

To find what service you need click on the Go To button and type it in. Alternatively **www.bt.com/phonenetuk** takes you right to the on-line phone book.

Fishing

see Sport

Fitness

see Health

Food and Drink

Whether you want to order from the comfort of your own home, indulge yourself, find the latest food news or get a recipe, this collection of sites will fulfil your foodie desires. It features supermarkets, on-line magazines and information sites, specialist food retailers, vegetarian, organic, drinks, kitchen equipment and eating out.

Supermarkets

www.icelandfreeshop.com
FROZEN FOOD SPECIALIST DELIVERS

ORIGIN UK
SPEED ✓✓✓
INFO ✓✓✓✓
VALUE ✓✓✓
EASE ✓✓✓✓

Iceland's service is good and nearly all of the UK is covered. Easy to navigate, but can be ponderous to use. Your order is saved each time which then acts as the basis for your next order. Information on the products is good, and orders must be £40 or more.

www.waitrose.co.uk
IF YOU ARE REALLY INTO FOOD

ORIGIN UK
SPEED ✓✓✓
INFO ✓✓✓✓✓
EASE ✓✓✓✓

Food retailer combined with Internet Service Provider, offering a comprehensive and well laid out site but you can't shop from the site yet. Has all the features you'd expect from an ISP, it also offers:

1. Access to the Carlton food network.
2. The excellent Waitrose Food Illustrated Magazine (also at www.wfi-online.com).
3. Waitrose Wine Direct.
4. Hardens Restaurant Guide.
5. The Raymond Blanc section with recipes and articles.
6. Investigate their shops in the John Lewis partnership.

www.tesco.co.uk
THE LIFESTYLE SUPERSTORE

ORIGIN UK
SPEED ✓✓✓
INFO ✓✓✓✓
VALUE ✓✓✓✓
EASE ✓✓✓✓

This functional site has the most comprehensive offering from the supermarkets. It has details of areas covered by their home delivery service which is similar to the Iceland service. Tesco are also an ISP

There is:
1. A well laid out bookshop.
2. Gift ideas.
3. A financial section with online banking.
4. An ideas for the Home section.
5. Tesco Online magazine.

www.sainsburys.co.uk
NOT JUST GOOD TASTE

ORIGIN UK
SPEED ✓✓✓✓
INFO ✓✓✓✓✓
VALUE ✓✓✓
EASE ✓✓✓✓

Sainsbury's site is similar, (but jollier) in content to Tesco, but without the financial advice. Entertaining to use, and much faster too, with the emphasis being on good food, cooking, recommendation and taste. Sainsburys are also an ISP
1. The "find a recipe" service is excellent.
2. There is a good "I want…" search facility.
3. Good section on organic food.
4. Great articles and recipes from the Sainsburys Magazine.

www.somerfield.co.uk
IMPRESSIVE

ORIGIN UK
SPEED ✓✓✓✓✓
INFO ✓✓✓
VALUE ✓✓✓
EASE ✓✓✓✓

A very fast site, which also features the Kwik Save stores. The home delivery section is up and running, seemingly going to more locations than the major supermarkets. Register for the promised 24-7 (**www.24-7.co.uk**) complete home shopping service too. The key sections are:
1. The latest savings.
2. Seasonal recipes.
3. Meals in minutes.
4. A store locator.
5. A "kids club".

www.asda.co.uk

VALUE MAD

ORIGIN	UK
SPEED	✓✓✓✓
INFO	✓✓
VALUE	✓✓✓✓✓
EASE	✓✓✓

An unattractive, poorly designed but simple to use site. One half is the basic Asda bit with information sections about:

1. The company, jobs and current store offers.
2. Under "what's new" is Asda@Home, a phone ordering service for books, CDs and videos.

The second half is **www.valuemad.com**, which is a site produced by Asda and partners. It's a price comparison tool that finds the cheapest price for a particular product and takes you to the retailer site to buy it. This site is disappointing but expect more from Asda in future.

www.safeway.co.uk

FOR THE FAMILY WITH YOUNG CHILDREN

ORIGIN	UK
SPEED	✓✓
INFO	✓✓✓✓
EASE	✓✓✓✓

Slow and worthy; you can't actually shop from the site yet, however its great strength is the section on the family, with lots of good advice for parents of young children. Also information about the company and loyalty card, a recipe finder and a pointless shopping list facility.

Specialist food retailers

www.curryhouse.co.uk

EVERYTHING YOU NEED TO KNOW ABOUT CURRY

ORIGIN	UK
SPEED	✓✓✓
INFO	✓✓✓✓✓
VALUE	✓✓✓
EASE	✓✓✓✓✓

Curryholics can get their fill of recipes, recommendations, taste tests, interviews with famous chefs and a restaurant guide. Spices and curry mixes can be bought from Chilli Willies online shop, all orders charged £2.99 p&p. See also **www.curryworld.com**.

www.heinz-direct.co.uk

DELIVERING MORE THAN 57 VARIETIES OF FOOD

ORIGIN UK	To get the best value for money it's best to order in
SPEED ✓✓	bulk, as delivery charges can be high. It can be very
INFO ✓✓✓	slow to use and is split into product feature sections:
VALUE ✓✓✓✓	1. Weight watchers.
EASE ✓✓✓✓	2. Canned grocery.

3. Heinz and Farley's baby food.
4. Hampers.
5. Sauces and pickles.

www.bluemango.co.uk

SPREADS THE WORD

ORIGIN UK	This highly acclaimed site sells everything that you
SPEED ✓✓✓✓	can spread. There are also offers, recipes and a list
INFO ✓✓✓✓✓	of links to other food retailers. Everything is well
VALUE ✓✓✓	explained, and the food on offer has ingredients
EASE ✓✓✓✓	listed. It's quick, easy-to-use and delivery is £4 per

order. It's split into:
1. Chutneys.
2. Curds.
3. Dips and salsas.
4. Honey.
5. Jams.
6. Gifts.

www.chocolatestore.com

LUXURY CHOCOLATES WORLDWIDE

ORIGIN UK	It's fast and easy-to-use with the UK shipping being
SPEED ✓✓✓✓	£1 per item. There is also a facility to send any page
INFO ✓✓✓✓	to a fellow chocoholic. Split into four areas:
VALUE ✓✓	1. Chocolate recipes.
EASE ✓✓✓✓	2. Gift section complete with greeting card service.

3. Product listing.

4. A forum "melting pot" for answers to any choccie related question.

www.thorntons.co.uk
WELCOME TO CHOCOLATE HEAVEN

ORIGIN UK
SPEED ✓✓✓✓
INFO ✓✓✓
VALUE ✓✓✓
EASE ✓✓✓✓

Thorntons offer a comprehensive and easy-to-use site, with an emphasis on selling. The range is extensive and they supply worldwide – at a cost. All orders are £3.95 for the UK. There are product sections for continental, premier, gifts and hampers. For kids there's a Winnie the Pooh section and access to a fairly bizarre add-on site called Thortons Natural Discovery – they should stick to chocolate.

www.cheese.com
IT'S ALL ABOUT CHEESE!

ORIGIN UK
SPEED ✓✓✓✓
INFO ✓✓✓
VALUE ✓✓✓
EASE ✓✓✓✓

Not a shop, but a huge resource site listing over 650 types of cheese. There's advice about the best way to eat cheese, a vegetarian section, a cheese bookshop and links to other cheese related sites and on-line stores. You can even find a suitable cheese, searching by texture, country or type of milk.

www.cheesemongers.co.uk
OPULENT SITE FROM UK'S OLDEST CHEESEMONGERS

ORIGIN UK
SPEED ✓✓✓✓
INFO ✓✓✓✓✓
EASE ✓✓✓✓

Paxton and Whitfield, the royal cheesemongers, provide a very clear and easy-to-use on-line shop but charge £7.50 to ship goods. A superb selection of cheese and luxury produce, with hampers, cheese kitchen, accessories and wine. A pleasure to browse and it's tempting to buy, you can also join the Cheese Society. See also **www.fromages.com** for French cheese with no delivery charge

www.teddingtoncheese.co.uk

BRITISH AND CONTINENTAL CHEESEMONGERS

ORIGIN UK
SPEED ✓✓✓
INFO ✓✓✓✓
VALUE ✓✓✓
EASE ✓✓✓✓

Much acclaimed site offering a wider variety of cheese than Paxton and Whitfield at slightly better prices. The sections are split by country and there's a good system for showing whether the cheese is suitable for vegetarians, pregnant women etc. There is also a small selection of wine and other produce. When buying you can stipulate how much cheese you want in grams (150 minimum), shipping is £5.95 for the UK.

www.realmeat.co.uk

DEDICATED TO PRODUCING THE SAFEST, KINDEST, TASTIEST MEAT.

ORIGIN UK
SPEED ✓✓✓✓
INFO ✓✓✓
VALUE ✓✓✓
EASE ✓✓✓✓

Family run concern that produces meat in a caring and compassionate way. There is a section about their philosophy, a magazine called the Real Meat Review and the on-line shop. The shop is split into several areas featuring different meat products, it's easy-to-use and shipping within the UK costs £3.95 per order.

www.stgeorgessquare.com

A VIRTUAL VILLAGE MARKET SQUARE

ORIGIN UK
SPEED ✓✓✓✓
INFO ✓✓✓
VALUE ✓✓✓
EASE ✓✓✓✓

St Georges Square features five shops:
1. A good wine store with several hundred wines.
2. An organics store with a good selection of produce.
3. A flower shop with a small selection of arrangements.
4. A wide range of themed hampers.

5. The food hall containing the best of British foods featuring specialist retailers in meat, cheese, biscuits, chocolates and preserves.

It's fast and easy-to-use, with some good offers too. Shipping is between £8 and £10 depending on the size of the order and type of goods you are buying.

www.homefarmfoods.com
DELICIOUS FROZEN FOOD DELIVERED FREE

ORIGIN UK	Good selection of frozen foods with a good use of symbols indicating whether the product is low fat, microwaveable or vegetarian etc. With free delivery, it's especially good value, and there is no minimum order. Sections on: meals for one, Chinese, Indian, puddings, family favourites.
SPEED ✓✓✓	
INFO ✓✓✓	
VALUE ✓✓✓✓✓	
EASE ✓✓✓✓	

www.pinneys-mail-order.co.uk
GOURMET GIFTS DELIVERED DIRECT

ORIGIN UK	This company specialises in quality Scottish foods, mainly salmon, trout and a selection of hampers. It's fast, easy-to-use and delivery is free in the UK. For a similar but slower offering also check out www.baxters.co.uk.
SPEED ✓✓✓✓	
INFO ✓✓✓	
VALUE ✓✓	
EASE ✓✓✓✓	

www.leapingsalmon.co.uk
STRESS IS FOR OTHER FISH

ORIGIN UK	This is about providing creative and inspirational products to make gourmet cooking fun and achievable in the home. Each meal kit is created for two people by a top chef with step-by-step instructions, order your meal the day before and it gets delivered overnight so that the food is as fresh as possible. They deliver anywhere in the UK for £4.50.
SPEED ✓✓✓✓	
INFO ✓✓✓✓✓	
VALUE ✓✓✓	
EASE ✓✓✓✓	

www.jayfruit.co.uk
LE GOURMET FRANÇAIS ONLINE

ORIGIN UK
SPEED ✓✓
INFO ✓✓✓✓
VALUE ✓✓
EASE ✓✓

The aim is to offer the finest imported lines, currently only available to the top chefs, for use in the home kitchen – there are some gorgeous things here. As the products on offer are special, it's a shame that the site is slow to use, and not good value. Orders must be over £20 and delivery is £4.99.

www.mailacake.co.uk
FOR ANY FESTIVITY, SPECIAL OCCASION, CELEBRATION OR TO TREAT YOURSELF

ORIGIN UK
SPEED ✓✓✓✓
INFO ✓✓
VALUE ✓✓
EASE ✓✓✓✓

You've only got one choice of rich 2lb fruitcake, albeit with two different toppings – cherries & nuts and marzipan & icing or you can have it plain too. Add any message you like and have it delivered in the UK for the all-inclusive price of £16.50. There's also a corporate service.

www.juliangraves.co.uk
THE FINEST FOODS FROM AROUND THE GLOBE

ORIGIN UK
SPEED ✓✓✓✓
INFO ✓✓
VALUE ✓✓✓
EASE ✓✓✓✓

A strong offering and easy-to-use, you can buy a large range of usual products as well as body-care products, vitamins, oils and confectionery. More detail about the products is needed and you need to buy in bulk to make it real value for money.

www.farmersmarkets.net
FARM-FRESH PRODUCTS

ORIGIN UK
SPEED ✓✓✓
INFO ✓✓✓
EASE ✓✓✓

Cut out the middle man and buy local, fresh produce direct from the farmer. Find out the location and times of your nearest market.

Recipes, general food sites and magazines

www.kitchenlink.com
YOUR GUIDE TO WHAT'S COOKING ON THE NET

ORIGIN US
SPEED ✓✓✓✓
INFO ✓✓✓✓✓
EASE ✓✓✓

A bit clunky to use, but it has so many links to other key foodie sites and food related sections that it has to be the place to start your on-line food and drink experience. The design can make it irritating to use, but persevere and you'll be rewarded with a resource that is difficult to beat. However, you can also try **www.cyber-kitchen.com**, which is nearly as comprehensive, but less fussy than Kitchen-link, with fun graphics and links to almost 5000 related web sites. The site is split into six main sections:
1. Cookery books.
2. Recipe exchange.
3. Links to related sites.
4. Recipes.
5. What's new in food.
6. A cookery search engine.

www.tudocs.com
THE ULTIMATE DIRECTORY OF COOKING SITES

ORIGIN US
SPEED ✓✓✓✓
INFO ✓✓✓✓✓
EASE ✓✓✓✓

The main difference with Tudocs is that it grades each cookery site on its site listing. The listing is divided up into 19 sections, such as meat, beverages, low fat and ethnic. British cookery is classed as ethnic.

http://epicurious.com
FOR PEOPLE WHO EAT

ORIGIN UK
SPEED ✓✓✓✓
INFO ✓✓✓✓✓
EASE ✓✓✓✓

Owned by Conde Nast, this massive site combines articles from their magazines with information generated by the Epicurious team. There are over 33 different sections such as recipe search, tips, a food dictionary, restaurant reviews, live chat, forums, wine and a kitchen equipment shop. It's fast, easy to navigate and international in feel. It also has an online travel agent – **www.concierge.com**.

www.foodlines.com

FOR PEOPLE WHO HAVE A PASSION FOR FOOD

ORIGIN CANADA	It's easy to find the right recipe at this comprehen-
SPEED ✓✓✓✓	sive site with a modern touch. It's Canadian but
INFO ✓✓✓✓	don't let that put you off; there are some good
VALUE ✓	recipes, as well as food quizzes and food jokes.
EASE ✓✓✓✓	

www.simplyfood.co.uk

FOR PEOPLE WHO LOVE GOOD EATING AND DRINKING

ORIGIN UK	This bright site is part of the Carlton Food network.
SPEED ✓✓✓✓	Updated daily, it features thousands of recipes, food
INFO ✓✓✓✓	news, reviews on the latest products, food and wine
VALUE ✓✓	matching, a restaurant search, nutritional informa-
EASE ✓✓✓✓	tion and competitions. There are links to related

sites and you can buy a limited amount of goods as well.

www.cookingindex.com

LINKING YOU TO THE WORLD OF GOOD FOOD

ORIGIN US	The aim of the cooking index is to provide a list of
SPEED ✓✓✓✓	all the latest and most useful food and drink related
INFO ✓✓✓✓✓	web sites. Although it is very American in feel, there
VALUE ✓	is a great deal here, such as the newsletter, free
EASE ✓✓✓✓	recipes and the link search facility.

Kitchen equipment

www.lakelandlimited.co.uk
EXCELLENT CUSTOMER SERVICE

ORIGIN UK	Lakeland pride themselves on service and it shows,
SPEED ✓✓✓✓	they aim to get all orders dispatched in 24 hours
INFO ✓✓✓✓	and delivery on orders over £35 is free. The
VALUE ✓✓✓	product listing for both kitchen and homeware is
EASE ✓✓✓✓	comprehensive. See also www.kitchenware.co.uk

www.pots-and-pans.co.uk
QUALITY SECONDS

ORIGIN UK	Scottish company offering kitchen equipment
SPEED ✓✓✓	through a good on-line store; it's good value but
INFO ✓✓✓✓	delivery charges may vary.
VALUE ✓✓✓✓	
EASE ✓✓✓✓	

Vegetarian and organic

www.organicfood.co.uk
A WORLD OF ORGANIC INFORMATION

ORIGIN UK	A very informative site which gives the latest news
SPEED ✓✓✓	on organic food. There is a message board, news, a
INFO ✓✓✓✓✓	quiz and recommendations on where to shop, both
EASE ✓✓✓✓	locally and on-line. There's also a herb guide.

www.organicsdirect.co.uk
NATIONWIDE 100% VEGETARIAN ORGANIC
HOME-DELIVERY

ORIGIN UK	Award winning and recommended by *You* magazine
SPEED ✓✓✓✓	amongst others, this company offers a wide variety
INFO ✓✓✓✓	of food in eight categories; fields & orchards, larder
VALUE ✓✓✓✓	& dairy, bakery, baby food, farmhouse kitchen,
EASE ✓✓✓✓	

juice bar, wine cellar and a general store. Much better value than supermarkets, delivery (UK) is £5.95 up to 20kg, with a further 25p a kilo after that.

www.purelyorganic.co.uk
THE ORGANIC SUPERMARKET

ORIGIN UK	Similar in scope to Organicsdirect but with more vari-
SPEED ✓✓✓	ety including organic meat. It also has information on
INFO ✓✓✓✓	other topics such as GM foods. Delivery charges are
VALUE ✓✓✓✓	£6 for orders under £70, with orders over £70 free.
EASE ✓✓✓✓	

www.freshfood.co.uk
WELCOME TO THE ORGANIC NATION

ORIGIN UK	Another combined supermarket and information
SPEED ✓✓	site, this one has a recipe section too. Similar to the
INFO ✓✓✓	last two sites but slower to use. Delivery charges are
VALUE ✓✓✓✓	£5 for a minimum order of £30 with discounts if
EASE ✓✓	you subscribe to a regular order.

www.veg.org
THE INTERNET'S DEFINITIVE GUIDE FOR VEGETARIANS

ORIGIN UK	A huge resource site that covers everything a vege-
SPEED ✓✓✓✓	tarian could want to know, it has an easy-to-use
INFO ✓✓✓✓✓	database and is international in scope. There are
EASE ✓✓✓✓	hundreds of links to related sites.

www.vegsoc.org
THE VEGETARIAN SOCIETY

ORIGIN UK	This is the official site of the UK branch and is split
SPEED ✓✓✓✓✓	into ten sections: news, new veggies, environment,
INFO ✓✓✓✓✓	business opportunities, recipes and the Cordon Vert
VALUE ✓✓	school, youth with virtual schoolroom, health,
EASE ✓✓✓✓	

membership info and on-line bookstore. Each
section is packed with information, written in plain
English, and there is a search engine for information
on any veggie topic.

www.vegweb.com
VEGGIES UNITE!

ORIGIN US
SPEED ✓✓✓
INFO ✓✓✓✓✓
VALUE ✓✓
EASE ✓✓✓✓

If you're a vegetarian this is a great place. There are
hundreds of recipes, plus features and ideas in the
VegWeb newsletter. There's also a good bookshop
and a link to a grocery store www.wholefoods.com
whose site is informative, but they don't ship to the
UK. The whole thing is funded by a membership
subscription of $15.

www.vegansociety.com
PROMOTING WAYS OF LIVING WHICH AVOID THE USE OF ANIMAL PRODUCTS

ORIGIN UK
SPEED ✓✓✓✓
INFO ✓✓✓✓
VALUE ✓✓✓
EASE ✓✓✓✓

The official site of the Vegan Society, promotes
veganism by providing information, links to other
related sites and books. You can't shop from the site
but it does recommend suitable retailers.

Dieting

www.3fatchicks.com
THE SOURCE FOR DIET SUPPORT

ORIGIN US
SPEED ✓✓✓✓
INFO ✓✓✓✓✓
VALUE ✓✓✓
EASE ✓✓✓✓✓

The awesome Three Fat Chicks have produced one
of the best food web sites. It's entertaining and
informative about dieting or trying to stay healthy.
There are food reviews, how to live on fast food,
recipes, links to other low fat sites, a section for
chocoholics, diet tips and "tool box" which has

calorie tables and calculators; also getting started on losing weight and how to get free samples.

www.cookinglight.com

THE BEST FROM COOKING LIGHT MAGAZINE

ORIGIN US	One of the world's best selling food magazines, their
SPEED ✓✓	site offers a huge selection of healthy recipes and
INFO ✓✓✓	step-by-step guides to cooking. There are also
EASE ✓✓✓✓	articles on healthy living.

http://uk.weightwatchers.com

WELCOME TO WEIGHTWATCHERS UK

ORIGIN UK	A site designed to plug their product rather than to
SPEED ✓✓✓✓	offer genuine on-line advice, although there are
INFO ✓✓	some recipes available. An opportunity missed, as
VALUE ✓	the site could have been much more pro-active.
EASE ✓✓✓✓	

www.mynutrition.co.uk

ON-LINE GUIDE TO HEALTHY EATING

ORIGIN UK	Find out what you really should be eating from this
SPEED ✓✓✓✓	cool British site, which has been put together by a
INFO ✓✓✓	professional nutritionist. It features:
VALUE ✓✓	
EASE ✓✓✓✓	

1. Myconditions – an alphabetical listing of diseases and ailments with a short description of what effect they have on the diet, and advice on dietary needs and supplements.
2. Mynews – a newsletter with all the latest information on nutrition.
3. Mylibrary – with articles and book excerpts by the sites author.
4. Myconsultation – fill in a questionnaire about your health and get the dietary advice on eating and supplements.
5. Mystuff – records how you get on after the

consultation so that when you revisit you can check on progress.

6. Myshopping – buy those vitamins and supplements that have been recommended. Delivery is £2 for the UK. For all its beauty and efficiency, you can't help thinking that this is just a vehicle for selling vitamins and supplements.See also the Health section on page 109.

Drink

www.thebevnet.com

FOR NON-ALCOHOLICS ONLY

ORIGIN US	Short for the Beverage Network, the idea is to test
SPEED ✓✓	non-alcoholic soft drinks and to provide a written
INFO ✓✓✓✓	critique of each. There are some 700 listed, sadly
EASE ✓✓✓✓	you can't order them for the UK, The fun of the
	site is spoilt, by too much advertising, and it's
	quite slow.

www.whittard.com

OVER 150 FINEST SPECIALITY TEAS DELIVERED WORLDWIDE

ORIGIN UK	Good selection of teas, coffees and related products,
SPEED ✓✓	some 450 in all. It's not especially fast, but it's easy-
INFO ✓✓✓✓	to-use and they will ship throughout the world;
VALUE ✓✓✓	delivery is £3.95 for the UK. Also information on
EASE ✓✓✓✓	tea, coffee and making the perfect cuppa.

www.camra.org

THE CAMPAIGN FOR REAL ALE STARTS HERE

ORIGIN UK	A comprehensive site that has all the news and views
SPEED ✓✓✓	on the campaign for real ale. Sadly, it only advertises
INFO ✓✓✓	its Good Beer Guide and local versions, with only a
EASE ✓✓✓✓	

small section on the best beers. Includes sections on
beer in Europe, cider and festivals.

*There are many web sites selling wine and spirits, these are the
best so far.*

www.berry-bros.co.uk or www.bbr.co.uk
THE INTERNET WINE SHOP

ORIGIN UK	This attractive site offers over 1000 different wines
SPEED ✓✓✓	and spirits at prices from £3 to over £600. There is a
INFO ✓✓✓✓✓	great deal of information about each wine and a
VALUE ✓✓	good personal feel to the site. You can also buy
EASE ✓✓✓✓	related products such as cigars. Delivery for orders

over £100 is free, otherwise it's £7.50 for the UK.
They will deliver abroad and even store the wine for
you.

www.winecellar.co.uk
NOT JUST WINE AND GOOD VALUE

ORIGIN UK	They also sell spirits as well as wine and, while the
SPEED ✓✓✓✓	choice isn't as good as some on-line wine retailers,
INFO ✓✓✓✓	Wine Cellar are good value. Delivery is free for
VALUE ✓✓✓✓	orders of 12 bottles or more, otherwise it's £3.99.
EASE ✓✓✓	

www.drinks-direct.co.uk
GIFTS FOR ANY OCCASION

ORIGIN UK	If you want to give wine, chocolates, flowers or a
SPEED ✓✓✓✓	hamper then Drinks Direct is for you. The accent is
INFO ✓✓	on gifts so the wine selection isn't large, and delivery
VALUE ✓✓✓✓	costs £5.99 but includes gift-wrapping. If you live in
EASE ✓✓✓	London or the Midlands they will organise a wine

tasting party for you.

www.enjoyment.co.uk

IF YOU ENJOY WINE, THEN YOU'RE IN THE RIGHT PLACE TO SHOP

ORIGIN UK	Enjoyment is run by the company who own
SPEED ✓✓✓	Oddbins, Threshers and Victoria Wine stores. It's a
INFO ✓✓✓✓	fun site with over 800 wines to choose from with
VALUE ✓✓✓✓	good information on each one. It's good value too
EASE ✓✓✓	with discounts of up to 15% on the high street
	price. Deliveries costs £4.99.

www.chateauonline.co.uk

THE WINE SPECIALIST ON THE INTERNET

ORIGIN UK	This much advertised retailer offers some 800 wines,
SPEED ✓✓✓	and if you know a bit about wine then this is a good
INFO ✓✓✓✓✓	site, with lots of expert advice and recommendation.
VALUE ✓✓✓	They claim to be up to 30% cheaper than other
EASE ✓✓✓✓✓	wine retailers, but you really have to order 12
	bottles. Delivery is £5.99 for the UK.

www.wine-lovers-page.com

ONE OF THE BEST PLACES TO LEARN ABOUT WINE

ORIGIN US	Highly informative for novices and experts alike,
SPEED ✓✓✓✓	this site has it all. There are categories on learning
INFO ✓✓✓✓✓	about wine, reading and buying books and tasting
VALUE ✓✓✓	notes for some 50,000 wines. Also within the 28
EASE ✓✓✓	sections there's a wine search engine and much
	more.

www.winespectator.com

THE MOST COMPREHENSIVE WINE WEB SITE

ORIGIN UK	From *Wine Spectator* magazine you get a site
SPEED ✓✓✓	packed with information. There are eleven
INFO ✓✓✓✓✓	comprehensive sections: news, features, a wine
EASE ✓✓✓✓	search facility, forums, weekly features, a library, the

best wineries, wine auctions and travel. The dining section has a world restaurant guide, tips on eating out, wine matching and a set of links to gourmet food. You can subscribe to the whole site, which includes access to their archive material for $29.95 a month.

www.wine-pages.com

A GREAT BRITISH NON-COMMERCIAL WINE SITE

ORIGIN UK
SPEED ✓✓✓
INFO ✓✓✓✓✓
EASE ✓✓✓

Most independently written wine sites are poor, however wine expert Tom Cannavan has put together a strong offering, which is updated daily. It's well written, informative and links to other good wine sites and on-line wine merchants. For another good British independent wine site, try the Wine Anorak at www.geocities.com/NapaValley/6576/antit.html.

www.drinkboy.com

ADVENTURES IN COCKTAILS

ORIGIN US
SPEED ✓✓✓✓
INFO ✓✓✓✓
EASE ✓✓✓✓✓

You can't shop from this site, but it contains virtually everything you need to know about the cocktails including instructions for around 100. There is also a section in the making on party games.

www.barmeister.com

THE ON-LINE GUIDE TO DRINKING

ORIGIN US
SPEED ✓✓✓
INFO ✓✓✓✓
EASE ✓✓✓✓

Packed with information on everything to do with drink, there are over 1300 drink recipes available and over 400 drinking games. If you have another, then send yours to be featured in the site.

Eating out

www.goodguides.com
HOME OF THE GOOD PUB GUIDE

ORIGIN UK
SPEED ✓✓✓✓
INFO ✓✓✓✓
EASE ✓✓✓✓

Once you've registered it has an easy-to-use regional guide to the best pubs, which are rated on food, beer, value, good place to stay and good range of wine. You can also get a listing by award winner. It also houses the Good Guide to Britain, which is a good resource for what's on where.

www.dine-online.co.uk
UK BASED WINING, DINING AND TRAVEL REVIEW

ORIGIN UK
SPEED ✓✓✓✓
INFO ✓✓✓✓
VALUE ✓
EASE ✓✓✓✓

A slightly pretentious, but a sincere attempt at an independent eating out review web site. It has a good selection of recommended restaurants, covers wine and has some good feature articles. It relies heavily on reader recommendation.

www.restaurants.co.uk
FIND THE RIGHT PLACE TO EAT, ANYWHERE IN THE UK

ORIGIN UK
SPEED ✓✓✓
INFO ✓✓✓✓
EASE ✓✓

A confusing site that lists nearly all the UK's restaurants from pits to palaces. You can add your review or go to another review site, but on the whole it doesn't recommend. There are also sections on catering suppliers, recipes and pub food. There's a drive to get advertising on the site, and it is a little out-of-date.

www.theaa.co.uk/hotels/index.asp
NOT JUST MOTORING AND TRAVEL ADVICE

ORIGIN UK
SPEED ✓✓✓✓
INFO ✓✓✓✓✓
EASE ✓✓✓✓✓

The superb AA site has a little known gem in its hotels section – an excellent regional restaurant guide to the UK. Each hotel and restaurant is graded and there are comments on quality of food, ambience, an idea of the price and, of course, how to get there.

Two sites to watch which aren't quite up to speed yet are **www.cuisinenet.co.uk** *and* **www.local-restaurant.com** *Both make recommendations and will allow you to search for restaurants.*

Fun

see Humour

Furniture

see DIY and Home

Free Stuff

Free stuff is exactly what the term suggests, and these are sites whose owners have trawled the net or been offered free services, software, trial products and so on. It's amazing what you can find but as most sites are American some offers won't apply.

www.allforfree.co.uk

DELIVERED DAILY IN YOUR E-MAIL

ORIGIN UK
SPEED ✓✓
INFO ✓✓✓✓✓
VALUE ✓✓✓✓✓
EASE ✓✓✓✓

All for free will let you know all the latest "free" news with their e-mail service. There's a lot here, the highlights being how to ensure that you are getting the most out of government services, free internet access, free magazines and where to go for the best competitions. You could also try **www.thefreezone.co.uk**, which is less cluttered – and less available; it's more of a collection of link pages that is worth persevering with.

www.free.com
GET SOMETHING FOR NOTHING

ORIGIN	US
SPEED	✓✓✓
INFO	✓✓✓✓✓
VALUE	✓✓✓✓✓
EASE	✓✓✓✓✓

One of the best and largest sites of its type, there are literally hundreds of pages of free goodies waiting to be snapped up. Very wide-ranging and very much geared towards the US. See also **www.1freestuff.com** or **www.freeandfun.com**, or **www.totallyfreestuff.com**, which are all very similar American sites. Also **www.thefreesite.com** which is consistently faster than the others.

Galleries

see Art

Games and Gambling

Gambling sites abound on the internet and they often use some of the most sophisticated marketing techniques to keep you hooked, new screens pop up as you click on the close button tempting you with the chance to win millions. All the gaming sites are monitored by gaming commissions but above all be sensible: it's easy to get carried away. If you don't fancy playing with your own money or just like to play games for the fun of it, there are many good sites available. Remember to read the rules of each game thoroughly, especially for the multi-player games.

www.national-lottery.co.uk
IT COULD BE YOU

ORIGIN	UK
SPEED	✓✓
INFO	✓✓✓✓
EASE	✓✓✓✓

Find out about Camelot, good causes, the national lottery and whether you've won. Also, find out whether your premium bonds are worth anything at **www.nationalsavings.co.uk** you need your bond-holder number handy.

www.jamba.co.uk
WHERE THE WEB IS FUN

ORIGIN UK
SPEED ✓✓✓
INFO ✓✓✓✓
VALUE ✓✓✓✓
EASE ✓✓✓✓

Owned by Carlton TV, this is probably the most complete set of games and trivia, there's also a gaming section and you can place bets or go shopping as well. You have to register to take part in the prize-winning games.

www.prizes.com
FREE INSTANT WIN GAMES

ORIGIN US
SPEED ✓✓✓✓
INFO ✓✓✓
VALUE ✓✓✓✓✓
EASE ✓✓✓✓✓

Basically free on-line scratch-cards, you can win cash or play for tokens that you can later exchange for cash.

www.24ktgoldcasino.com
THE ON-LINE CASINO

ORIGIN US
SPEED ✓✓✓✓
INFO ✓✓✓✓
EASE ✓✓✓✓

Excellent graphics and fast response times make this great fun, but you need a decent PC to download the software. It is regulated just like any other casino and the odds are the same. There are 28 games and you can either play for fun or for money. For a similar experience but with slightly different games try **www.intercasino.com** who say they're the safest bet on the internet.

www.ukbetting.com
LIVE INTERACTIVE BETTING

ORIGIN UK
SPEED ✓✓✓✓
INFO ✓✓✓✓
EASE ✓✓✓✓

Concentrating on sports betting, this is a clear, easy-to-use site; take a guest tour before applying to join. You need to open an account to take part, using your credit or debit card, bets are £1 minimum.

The heavily advertised, and fun **www.bluesq.com**

also offers a simliar service, but with a football bias and special bets on things like soap operas, presidential elections and *Who Wants To Be A Millionaire?* See also www.inter-bet.com, which is easy-to-use, with loads of options and is probably better value than most sites.

www.bet.co.uk and www.ladbrokes.com
UK's NUMBER 1 BOOKMAKER

ORIGIN UK
SPEED ✓✓
INFO ✓✓✓✓
EASE ✓✓✓✓

Ladbrokes offer a combination of news, information and betting with the bet.co.uk site, which is geared almost entirely to football. The main site also has football, but also excellent features on racing, golf and the other major sports and sporting events. See also www.racingpost.co.uk who offer a similar combination of news and betting.

www.williamhill.co.uk or www.willhill.com
THE MOST RESPECTED NAME IN BOOKMAKING

ORIGIN UK
SPEED ✓✓✓✓
INFO ✓✓✓✓
EASE ✓✓✓✓✓

The best on-line betting site in terms of speed, layout and design, it has the best event finder, results service and betting calculator. The bet finder service is also very good and quick. All the major sports are featured and there is a specials section for those out of the ordinary flutters.

www.tote.co.uk
BET ON THE HORSES, LIVE

ORIGIN UK
SPEED ✓✓✓✓
INFO ✓✓✓✓
EASE ✓✓✓✓

Devoted to horse racing, the Tote fairly successfully attempts to bring you the excitement and feel of using the on-line betting, what the bets mean and a very good set of links relating to horses and racing.

www.thedogs.co.uk
GONE TO THE DOGS

ORIGIN	UK ✓✓✓
SPEED	✓✓✓
INFO	✓✓✓✓✓
EASE	✓✓✓✓

Everything you need to know about greyhounds and greyhound racing, you can adopt or get advice on buying a dog, find the nearest track, and learn how to place bets. You can't gamble from the site though there are links to other on-line bookies.

Games

www.riddler.com
LOTS TO THINK ABOUT

ORIGIN	US
SPEED	✓✓✓✓
INFO	✓✓✓✓
EASE	✓✓✓✓

Excellent for crosswords, solitaire and trivia, the response time on the games is very good, but the site is slowed down by the excessive advertising. To play in the multi-player games you need to register. You can win prizes but there is no gambling.

http://games.yahoo.com
PLAY OTHERS FOR FREE

ORIGIN	UK
SPEED	✓✓✓✓
INFO	✓✓✓✓✓
EASE	✓✓✓✓

The best for a wide selection of free games, including all the favourites, it's easy to register and play and you can be anonymous. Chatting to your opponent is part of the fun though and it's easy. There's also a good selection for the single player, particularly word games. AOL users may find it slow.

www.ogl.org
ONLINE GAMING LEAGUE

ORIGIN	US
SPEED	✓✓✓
INFO	✓✓✓✓
EASE	✓✓✓

This site provides an on-line competitive gaming league or ladder for many of the most popular PC games such as Quake, Arena and Tribes. It can be a little slow but it's easy to get involved.

www.test.com
INTERNET'S LARGEST COLLECTION OF INSTANTLY SCORED TESTS

ORIGIN US
SPEED ✓✓✓✓
INFO ✓✓✓✓✓
VALUE ✓
EASE ✓✓✓✓

This site takes testing seriously, you can brush up on exams or just test your mental agility, get your personality profiled or join MENSA www.mensa.org.uk. You have to pay for many of the tests although if you add your own test you get 50% of the revenue.

www.coolquiz.com
THE WEBSITE THAT KEEPS YOU GUESSING

ORIGIN US
SPEED ✓✓✓✓
INFO ✓✓✓✓
EASE ✓✓✓✓

Knowledge of trivia, entertainment, sports and American culture is a must. There are lots of different quizzes and you can set your own or challenge the Quizmaster. For a more British approach to trivia try www.quiz.co.uk.

www.chess.co.uk
THE HOME OF THE LONDON CHESS CENTRE

ORIGIN UK
SPEED ✓✓✓✓
INFO ✓✓✓✓
VALUE ✓✓✓
EASE ✓✓✓

Everything you need to know about chess on one site, it has links to other chess organisations, you can buy books, software and videos from the on-line store. There are also links to backgammon and bridge sites and organisations. Unfortunately you can't play, for that try Yahoo or go to www.chessed.com where you can play on-line.

www.cluemaster.com
HOME OF PUZZLES ON THE INTERNET

ORIGIN UK
SPEED ✓✓✓
INFO ✓✓✓✓
VALUE ✓✓✓✓
EASE ✓✓✓✓

For crossword and puzzle addicts, this site offers the ultimate fix. There are puzzles for all ages but the cryptic ones are up to broadsheet standard, some are interactive. In all there are over 1000 puzzles and they are all free.

www.mattelscrabble.com
THE HOME OF SCRABBLE

ORIGIN UK
SPEED ✓✓✓✓
INFO ✓✓✓✓
EASE ✓✓✓✓

Information on the UK's Scrabble scene, records, web links combined with a products listing and a few quizzes based on the game. You can't play the game itself though, for that you have to buy the CD.

www.thehouseofcards.com
THE BEST OF PLAYING CARDS

ORIGIN US
SPEED ✓✓✓✓
INFO ✓✓✓✓
VALUE ✓✓✓✓
EASE ✓✓✓✓

Excellent site featuring virtually every card game you can think of, it's particularly good on solitaire. There are links to other card web sites and free downloads of card games. You can play on-line or by yourself all for nothing or go to the shop and buy a game or two. There's also a good children's section.

www.winbridge.com
BRIDGE 24 HOURS A DAY

ORIGIN US
SPEED ✓✓✓
INFO ✓✓✓✓
EASE ✓✓✓✓

Get your fix here, along with 8000 other bridge addicts. There's also information on the game, the scoring, chat forums and a service to page you for a game.

www.bkgm.com
BACKGAMMON GALORE!

ORIGIN US
SPEED ✓✓✓✓
INFO ✓✓✓✓
VALUE ✓✓✓✓
EASE ✓✓✓✓

Devoted solely to backgammon, information, tips, links and downloads all free.

www.fantasyleague.com

FANTASY FOOTBALL IS NOW ON THE INTERNET

ORIGIN UK	Play and win up to £10,000, the site offers the ulti-
SPEED ✓✓✓✓	mate in fantasy football games and other spin offs;
INFO ✓✓✓✓	play either solo or with others. Also information on
EASE ✓✓✓✓	the players in "who's hot and who's not" and their
	real life clubs too.

Buying games

www.gamespy.com

FOR ALL THE LATEST GAMING NEWS

ORIGIN US	If you want to keep up with what's going on in the
SPEED ✓✓✓✓	gaming world here's the place to be. Vote on your
INFO ✓✓✓✓✓	favourite games, check out the hall of fame and get
VALUE ✓✓✓	the latest tips and downloads. You can also
EASE ✓✓✓✓	subscribe to their free newsletter.

www.gamesdomain.co.uk

BRITISH GAME NEWS AND REVIEWS

ORIGIN UK	A comprehensive site with lots to offer in terms of
SPEED ✓✓✓✓	reviews, downloads, resources and cheat tips, also
INFO ✓✓✓✓	offers freebies and on-line games.
VALUE ✓✓✓	
EASE ✓✓✓✓	

www.gameparadise.co.uk

TRUE PARADISE FOR GAME PLAYERS

ORIGIN UK	Excellent selection of games for all types of PCs,
SPEED ✓✓✓✓	with some good offers. There are also reviews and
INFO ✓✓✓✓	features with what's coming and tips on how to
VALUE ✓✓✓	play. You can also buy hardware at probably the
EASE ✓✓✓✓	best of the WH Smith on-line shops. Delivery is
	charged at 15% of what you buy up to £6
	maximum. For another similar site, try
	www.gamesstreet.co.uk.

www.ukgames.com
GAMES DISCOUNTED

ORIGIN UK
SPEED ✓✓✓✓
INFO ✓✓✓
VALUE ✓✓✓
EASE ✓✓✓

Good all rounder with over 2500 discounted products. It has features, demos, tips and great offers. Delivery charges can be a little steep and the best offers are reserved for members. See also **www.chipsworld.co.uk** who have good offers and free delivery for the UK.

www.classicgaming.com
GAMING AS YOU REMEMBER IT

ORIGIN UK
SPEED ✓✓✓✓
INFO ✓✓✓
VALUE ✓✓✓
EASE ✓✓

A web site that specialises in saving old consul games of yesteryear, (the 90s), it has hundreds of games to download, advice on how to play and a mission to re-unite people with their favourites with links to specialist sites.

See also **www.telegames.co.uk** who, apart from all the latest releases, have a good range of games for Ataris and older formats.

www.wireplay.com
DOWNLOAD FAVOURITE BOARD GAMES

ORIGIN UK
SPEED ✓✓✓✓
INFO ✓✓✓✓
VALUE ✓✓✓✓
EASE ✓✓✓✓

This excellent site from Gameplay offers free downloads of games including chess, Quake, X-wing Alliance, Jedi Knight and many more. You need to download the wireplay software and play on-line.

For a similar service also offering games with an educational leaning, try **www.dareware.com**. For another set of freebies and downloads go to **www.gamesdomain.com** a magazine spin off that also has over 1700 games reviews and previews. At the Tucows site **http://easynet.games.tucows.com** there's masses of free games, the highlight being the casino download.

For the top brands go to
www.nintendo.com
www.sega-europe.com
www.playstation.com
www.dreamcast.com
For children's games see Children's section
page 32.

Gardening

Many gardening sites are based in America, so bear this in mind for tenderness, soil and climate advice. Sites recommended give good general information and good links to specialist sites. Due to regulations on importing of seeds and plants you can't buy them from sites outside the UK.

www.gardenworld.co.uk
THE UK'S BEST

ORIGIN UK
SPEED ✓✓✓✓
INFO ✓✓✓✓
VALUE ✓✓✓
EASE ✓✓✓✓

Described as the UK's "best" garden centre and horticultural site. It includes a listing of over 600 garden centres, with addresses, contact numbers and e-mail. Outstanding list of links to other sites on other aspects of gardening. Truly comprehensive with sections on wildlife, books, holidays, advice, societies and specialists. However, it lacks a good plant finder service.

www.oxalis.co.uk
THE BIGGEST UK SITE – BRITISH GARDENING ON-LINE

ORIGIN UK
SPEED ✓✓
INFO ✓✓✓✓
VALUE ✓✓✓✓
EASE ✓✓

Oxalis is comprehensive, but cumbersome to use. It features gardens to visit, what's on, weather reports, a plant selector and an archive of articles written by members of the Garden Writers Guild.

www.gardenweb.com
GARDEN QUESTIONS ANSWERED

ORIGIN UK
SPEED ✓✓✓✓
INFO ✓✓✓✓✓
EASE ✓✓✓✓

Probably the best site for lively gardening debate; It's enjoyable, international, comprehensive with a nice tone. There are several discussion forums on various gardening topics, garden advice, plant dictionary and competitions such as guess the mystery plant. Using the forums is easy and fun, and you're sure to find the answer to almost any gardening question.

www.garden.com
A US SITE BUT ALSO GOOD FOR THE UK

ORIGIN US
SPEED ✓✓✓✓
INFO ✓✓✓✓✓
EASE ✓✓✓✓

A huge US based site with lots of relevant information and links for the British gardener. To get the best out of it, join the free membership, which gives use of advice service, use of a garden planner service, newsletter and a personalised garden notebook. The shop is not open to UK residents. Particularly fast to use if you're with AOL, not so with other ISPs.

www.igarden.co.uk
THE WEB GARDEN MAGAZINE

ORIGIN UK
SPEED ✓✓✓✓
INFO ✓✓✓✓✓
EASE ✓✓✓✓

Subscribe to the excellent Internet Garden Magazine for a host of features: news, advice, competitions, gardening links, retailers, information on courses, reader's offers and a good article archive library. Many of the best features are available to non-subscribers too. Another very good garden magazine is **www.plants-magazine.com**, broad in scope but particularly strong on new plants.

http://fff.nhm.ac.uk/fff
FLORA FOR FAUNA

ORIGIN UK	Using the postcode search, find out the plants that
SPEED ✓✓✓	are native to your area, where to get seeds and then
INFO ✓✓✓✓✓	how to look after them once they're in your garden.
EASE ✓✓✓	Sponsored by the Natural History Museum.

www.herbnet.com
GROWING, COOKING HERBS, GOOD LINKS

ORIGIN US	An American network specialising in herbs, with
SPEED ✓✓✓	links to specialists, trade and information sites.
INFO ✓✓✓✓	It can be hard work to negotiate, but there's no
EASE ✓✓✓	doubting the quality of the content.

www.flowerbase.com
FLOWERFINDER EXTRAORDINARY

ORIGIN HOL	Part of a Dutch network of sites called
SPEED ✓✓✓✓	"Flowerweb". An excellent resource for plantfinders
INFO ✓✓✓✓	enabling you to look up any plant and get its
EASE ✓✓✓✓	picture; it searches on part words.

www.gardenguides.com
HINTS AND TIPS

ORIGIN US	A useful American resource site with loads of infor-
SPEED ✓✓✓✓	mation on every aspect of gardening. It has lots of
INFO ✓✓✓✓	tips, handy guides, and a free on-line newsletter.
EASE ✓✓✓✓	

Gas

see Utilities

Genealogy

www.sog.org.uk
THE SOCIETY OF GENEALOGISTS

ORIGIN UK
SPEED ✓✓✓✓
INFO ✓✓✓✓
EASE ✓✓✓✓

This is the first place to go when you're thinking about researching your family tree. It won't win awards for web design, but it contains basic information and there is an excellent set of links you can use to start you off.

www.brit-a-r.demon.co.uk
THE OFFICIAL BRITISH ANCESTRAL RESEARCH SITE

ORIGIN UK
SPEED ✓✓✓✓
INFO ✓✓✓
VALUE ✓✓
EASE ✓✓✓✓

For £375 they will research one surname or line, for £675 two or a minimum of 6 hours work for £140. They guarantee results to four generations. Not as much fun as doing it yourself though.

www.genuki.org.uk
VIRTUAL LIBRARY OF GENEALOGICAL INFORMATION

ORIGIN UK
SPEED ✓✓✓✓
INFO ✓✓✓
EASE ✓✓✓✓

An excellent British oriented site with a huge range of links to help you find your ancestors. There is help for those starting out, news, bulletin boards, FAQs on genealogy and a regional search map of the UK and Ireland.

www.ancestry.com
No 1 SOURCE FOR FAMILY HISTORY

ORIGIN US
SPEED ✓✓✓✓
INFO ✓✓✓
VALUE ✓✓
EASE ✓✓✓✓

Find out about your ancestors for a $5 a month. This US oriented site has 500 million names and access to 2000 databases. It offers some information for free, but for real detail you have to join. It's especially good if you're searching for someone in the US or Canada.

www.surnameweb.org
ORIGINS OF SURNAMES

ORIGIN US	A great place to start your search for your family
SPEED ✓✓✓✓	origins. On top of the information about your name,
INFO ✓✓✓✓✓	there are thousands of links and they claim 2 billion
EASE ✓✓	searchable records.

Government

http://open.gov.co.uk
THE ENTRY POINT FOR GOVERNMENT INFORMATION

ORIGIN US	A massive web site devoted to the workings of our
SPEED ✓✓✓✓	government, it is a superb resource if you want to
INFO ✓✓✓✓✓	know anything official both at a national and a local
EASE ✓✓✓✓	level. Use the index or the search facility to navigate,

as it's easy to get side tracked. The top features are a
list of top 10 web sites, a monarchy section
www.royal.gov.uk, a download section and a feedback service.

Greetings Cards

www.intercarte.com
SEND A REAL CARD

ORIGIN UK	Prices start at £2.99 and delivery on orders placed
SPEED ✓✓✓	before 5pm will be posted via Royal Mail that day.
INFO ✓✓✓	The site features only Woodmansterne cards, and
EASE ✓✓✓	can be a little temperamental.

www.blue mountain.com
E-CARDS FOR FREE

ORIGIN UK	Great fun to use with a card for every occasion –
SPEED ✓✓✓	there are even cards for occasions you haven't heard
INFO ✓✓✓	
EASE ✓✓✓	

of. Also cards in several languages and cards with
music. See also **e-greetings.com**.

Gay/Lesbian

www.rainbownetwork.com
LESBIAN & GAY LIFESTYLE

ORIGIN UK	A very well thought out magazine-style web site
SPEED ✓✓✓✓	catering for all aspects of gay and lesbian life. It
INFO ✓✓✓✓✓	primarily covers news, fashion, entertainment and
EASE ✓✓✓✓	health. There are also forums and chat sections,
	classified ads as well as profiles on well-known
	personalities.

For other good gay/lesbian sites try:
www.gay.com – American magazine site
www.glinn.com – the gay gateway to the web
www.gaypride.co.uk – British site which is strong
    on links.

Health Advice

Here are some of the key sites for getting good health advice,
featuring on-line doctors, fitness centres, nutrition and sites that
try to combine all three. As with all health sites, there is no
substitute for the real thing and if you are ill, your main port of
call must be your doctor. Dietary advice sites are listed in the
food and drink section.

Health

www.nhsdirect.nhs.uk
THE NHS ONLINE

ORIGIN UK
SPEED ✓✓✓✓
INFO ✓✓✓✓✓
EASE ✓✓✓✓

NHS Direct is a telephone advice service and this is the internet spin off, with the emphasis on treating ailments at home. It comprises an excellent guide with audio clips, on a wide range of health topics and a superb selection of NHS-approved links covering specific illnesses or parts of the body. There's also health information and an A-Z guide to the NHS.

www.bupa.co.uk
BUPA HOMEPAGE

ORIGIN UK
SPEED ✓✓✓
INFO ✓✓✓✓✓
EASE ✓✓✓

Health fact-sheets, special offers on health cover, health tips and competitions are all on offer at this well designed site. You can also find your nearest BUPA hospital and instructions on referral.

www.healthfinder.com
A GREAT PLACE TO START FOR HEALTH ADVICE

ORIGIN US
SPEED ✓✓✓✓✓
INFO ✓✓✓✓✓
EASE ✓✓✓✓✓

Run by the US Department of Health, this provides a link to more or less every health organisation, medical and fitness site you can think of. In six sections you can learn about the hot medical topics, catch the medical news, make smart health choices, discover what's best for you and your lifestyle and use the medical dictionary in the research section. The site is well designed, fast and very easy-to-use.

www.patient.co.uk
FINDING INFORMATION FROM UK SOURCES

ORIGIN UK
SPEED ✓✓✓
INFO ✓✓✓✓✓
EASE ✓✓✓✓✓

This excellent site has been put together by two GPs. It's essentially a collection of links to other health sites, but from here you can find a web site on health-related topics with a UK bias. You can search alphabetically or browse within one of the nine key sections and there are a further twenty sub-sections. All the recommended sites are reviewed by a GP for suitability and quality before being placed on the site. For a second opinion, particularly on travel and complimentary medicine, go to **www.surgerydoor.co.uk** which is very good and is backed up by an on-line shop. Also try the well designed **www.netdoctor.co.uk** who describe themselves as the "UK's independent health web site" and offer a similar service.

www.medinex.com

THE SAFE HEALTH SEARCH

ORIGIN UK	An award winning site whose goal is to bring you
SPEED ✓✓✓✓	the best and most up-to-date information on health.
INFO ✓✓✓✓✓	It's done by partnering data from top doctors and
EASE ✓✓✓✓✓	organisations and making it available through one

search facility. Just fill in the form as you would a normal search engine and you get a list of articles and information on your chosen subject. There is almost too much information, and it would be good to have a search facility capable of narrowing down to a specific subject area.

www.drkoop.com

THE BEST PRESCRIPTION IS KNOWLEDGE

ORIGIN US	Don't let the silly name put you off, Dr C. Everett
SPEED ✓✓✓✓	Koop is a former US Surgeon General and is
INFO ✓✓✓✓✓	acknowledged as the best on-line doctor. The goal is
EASE ✓✓✓✓	to empower you to take care of your own health

through better knowledge. You have to register, but the site has all the latest health news plus:

1. A search engine that enables you to look up any health topic.
2. A family health advice section split for men, women, children and seniors.
3. Drug checker reassures and gives facts about medications. Links to an on-line drugstore.
4. The wellness section gives advice about fitness (both physical and mental), nutrition and offers a health check.
5. In Community you can chat on-line with fellow suffers and get support on a number of ailments.
6. An on-line medical encyclopaedia in the Conditions section, where you can look up any disease or symptom.

www.mayohealth.org

RELIABLE INFORMATION FOR A HEALTHY LIFE

ORIGIN US
SPEED ✓✓✓✓
INFO ✓✓✓✓✓
EASE ✓✓✓✓✓

Mayo has a similar ethic to Dr Koop and its site is less fussy and very easy-to-use. However, the amount of information can be overwhelming as they claim the combined knowledge of some 1200 doctors in the ten "centres". Essentially it's a massive collection of articles that combine to give you a large amount of data on specific medical topics.

www.quackwatch.com

HEALTH FRAUD, QUACKERY AND INTELLIGENT DECISIONS

ORIGIN US
SPEED ✓✓✓✓
INFO ✓✓✓✓
EASE ✓✓✓

Exposes fraudulent cures and old wives tales, then tells you where to get the right treatment. It makes fascinating reading and includes exposés on everything from acupuncture to weight loss. Use the search engine or just browse through it, many of the

articles leave you amazed at how fraudulent some
medical claims are.

www.onlinesurgery.com
ON-LINE OPERATIONS

ORIGIN US	Yes, you really can see live or recorded operations
SPEED ✓✓	providing you have RealPlayer.
INFO ✓✓✓✓	
EASE ✓✓✓	

www.allcures.com
UK'S FIRST ON-LINE PHARMACY

ORIGIN UK	After a fairly lengthy, but secure registration process
SPEED ✓✓✓	you can shop from the site which has all the big
INFO ✓✓✓✓	brands and a wide range of products. There are also
VALUE ✓✓✓	sections on toiletries, beauty, alternative medicine
EASE ✓✓✓	and a photo-shop. You can arrange to have your

prescriptions made up and sent to you with no delivery charge. See also **www.academyhealth.com** who
deliver free in the UK.

www.bodyisland.com
EVERYTHING FOR THE BODY ON ONE SITE

ORIGIN US	This is a concise and well put together site on keep-
SPEED ✓✓✓	ing healthy, all done with a nice dose of humour. It
INFO ✓✓✓✓	has six main subject areas: health, fitness, weight
VALUE ✓	loss, nutrition, relationships and female. In all six
EASE ✓✓✓	you can:

1. Visit a library that features articles on your
   chosen area.
2. Get advice from an expert.
3. Buy diet plans, books and nutrition software.
4. Enter discussion forums on a number of topics.
5. Find a list of links to other related sites including
   a UK section.

They will also help you with a good personal training program and if you are fit already there is a BodyIsland "pro" section just for you.

www.fitnesslink.com
FOR ALL THE NEWS THAT'S FIT!

ORIGIN US
SPEED ✓✓✓✓
INFO ✓✓✓✓
EASE ✓✓✓

Strongly American in tone and you almost expect it to whoop at you as you successfully navigate through its many subject areas. The key sections are:

1. In the Men's Locker room you can get advice on getting back into shape, muscle tone, how to meet gals at the gym or just look up the pin-up of the week.
2. In the Women's Locker room you too get a pin-up as well as advice on most aspects of exercise. There is a good section on exercises you can do after pregnancy or illness.

Joking aside this site offers excellent advice on exercise, especially those aimed at one body part.

www.fitnessonline.com
PROVIDING PERSONAL SUPPORT

ORIGIN US
SPEED ✓✓
INFO ✓✓✓✓✓
EASE ✓✓✓

This site is from an American magazine group. It takes a holistic view of health offering advice on exercise, nutrition and health products. In reality what you get is a succession of articles from their magazines, all are very informative but getting the right information can be time consuming.

www.drlockie.com
HOMEOPATHY MADE EASY

ORIGIN US
SPEED ✓✓✓
INFO ✓✓✓✓
EASE ✓✓✓✓✓

Click on any of the medicine jars to get what you need:

1. Information on homeopathy.

2. Details on homeopathic first-aid.
3. Treatments for many diseases and ailments.
4. Review and add to the list of Most Frequently
   Asked Questions on homeopathy.
5. Buy Dr Lockie's books via the Amazon bookstore.
6. Find links to other Homeopathic sites.
7. Search the site.

An interesting, clear and easy-to-use site
that offers sensible advice at all levels. See also
www.homeopathyhome.com.

Sites catering for a specific condition or disease

Here is a list of the key sites relating to specific diseases and
ailments, we have not attempted to review them, but if you know
of a site we've missed and would like it included in the next edition
of this book please e-mail us at **info@goodwebsiteguide.net.**

Alcohol and drug abuse
   www.drugnet.co.uk
   www.alcoholics-anonymous.org
   www.al-anon-alateen.org
Allergies
   www.allergy-info.com
Alzheimers
   www.alzheimers.org.uk
Aids and HIV
   www.tht.org.uk
   www.lovelife.hea.org.uk
Breast Cancer Campaign
   www.bcc-uk.org
Cancer
   www.cancerbacup.org
   www.crc.org.uk

Cerebral palsy
www.scope.org.uk
Dental
www.gdc-uk.org
Depression
www.gn.apc.org/da
Diabetics
www.diabetic.org.uk
Heart and Stroke
www.bhf.org.uk
www.stroke.org.uk
High blood pressure
www.hbpf.org.uk
Meningitis
www.meningitis-trust.org
Mental Health
www.mentalhealth.com
Quitting smoking
www.ash.org.uk
www.livesaver.co.uk
Stress
www.stressrelease.com

History and Biography

www.thehistorychannel.com
THE BEST SEARCH IN HISTORY

ORIGIN US
SPEED ✓✓✓✓
INFO ✓✓✓✓✓
EASE ✓✓✓

Excellent for history buffs, revision or just a good read the History Channel provides a site that is packed with information. Search by key word or timeline, and get biographical information, speeches, by date and by subject. It's fast and easy to get carried away once you start your search.

www.biography.com
FIND OUT ABOUT ANYONE WHO WAS ANYONE

ORIGIN US
SPEED ✓✓✓✓
INFO ✓✓✓✓✓
EASE ✓✓✓

Over 25,000 biographical references and some 2,500 videos make this site a great option if you need to find out about someone in a hurry. There are special features such as a book club and a magazine, there is a shop but at time of going to press they don't ship to the UK.

www.museumofcostume.co.uk
COSTUME THROUGH THE AGES

ORIGIN UK
SPEED ✓✓✓
INFO ✓✓✓✓
EASE ✓✓✓

Excellent site showing how the design of costume has changed through the ages. There's a virtual tour and links to other museums based in Bath.

Hobbies

www.yahoo.co.uk/recreation/hobbies
IF YOU CAN'T FIND YOUR HOBBY THEN LOOK HERE

ORIGIN UK
SPEED ✓✓✓✓
INFO ✓✓✓
VALUE ✓✓
EASE ✓✓✓✓

Hundreds of links for almost every conceivable pastime from amateur radio to urban exploration, it's part of the Yahoo service (see page 163); also see www.about.com who have a similarly large list but with an American bias.

www.cass-arts.co.uk
ONE STOP SHOP FOR ART MATERIALS

ORIGIN UK
SPEED ✓✓✓✓
INFO ✓✓✓
VALUE ✓✓
EASE ✓✓✓✓

A huge range of art and craft products available to buy on-line, also hints and tips and step-by-step guides for the novice. There is an on-line gallery and a section on art trivia and games. The shop has a decent search engine which copes with over 10,000 items, delivery is charged according to what you spend.

www.sewandso.co.uk
SHOP AT THE SPECIALISTS

ORIGIN UK
SPEED ✓✓✓
INFO ✓✓✓✓
VALUE ✓✓✓✓
EASE ✓✓✓✓

This site offers a huge range of kits and patterns for cross-stitch, needlepoint and embroidery. In addition, there's an equally large range of needle and threads. There are some good offers and delivery is only £1 for the UK, £6.50 to ship abroad.

www.horology.com
THE INDEX

ORIGIN US
SPEED ✓✓✓✓
INFO ✓✓✓
EASE ✓✓✓

The complete exploration of time, this is essentially a set of links for the committed horologist. It's pretty comprehensive, so if your hobby is tinkering about with clocks and watches, then this is a must.

www.royalmint.com
THE VALUE OF MONEY

ORIGIN UK
SPEED ✓✓✓✓
INFO ✓✓✓✓✓
VALUE ✓✓✓
EASE ✓✓✓✓

The Royal Mint's web site is informative, providing a history of the Mint, and coins themselves plus details on the coins they've issued. You can buy from the site and delivery is free. For coin news and valuations try **www.coin-news.com** or **www.coin-universe.com** all have good lists of links to specialist sites.

www.stangib.com
STAMPS ETC.

ORIGIN UK
SPEED ✓✓✓✓
INFO ✓✓✓
VALUE ✓✓✓
EASE ✓✓✓✓

The best prices and a user-friendly site for philatelists, you can buy a whole collection or sell them your own. Their catalogue is available on-line, and you can take part in auctions. See also **www.corbitts.com** who auction stamps, coins, notes and medals. **www.stamps.co.uk** is under construction, but will be an on-line resource site

for stamp collectors. For good prices see also
www.robinhood-stamp.co.uk.

www.towerhobbies.com
EXCITING WORLD OF RADIO CONTROLLED MODELLING

ORIGIN UK
SPEED ✓✓✓✓
INFO ✓✓✓
VALUE ✓✓✓
EASE ✓✓✓✓

An excellent, clearly laid out site offering a vast
range of radio-controlled models along with thousands of accessories and parts. The delivery charge
depends on the size of the order. For comparative
prices see **www.hobby-hobby.com**.

Holidays

see Travel

Homework

see Reference and Education

Horoscopes

see Astrology

Humour

www.funny.co.uk
THE COMEDY WEB DIRECTORY

ORIGIN UK
SPEED ✓✓✓
INFO ✓✓✓✓
EASE ✓✓✓✓

Here fun web sites are rated and collated, along with
news on who's doing what and where. There are
plenty of jokes, and if you register you can post your
own and subscribe to their magazine. For a laugh,
join the chat in their forum. This well-designed site
is spoiled by the large amount of advertising. For

loads of jokes go to www.jokepost.com, or
www.jokecenter.com, or www.jokes2000.com, or
www.funnybone.com.

www.amused.com
The Swiss Army knife of humour sites

ORIGIN US
SPEED ✓✓✓✓
INFO ✓✓✓✓
EASE ✓✓✓✓

News, jokes, stories, games, trivia, satire and
revenge it's all here in what is probably the most
comprehensive fun site. There is also a really good
set of links to other humour sites.

www.comedycentral.com
The home of South Park and more

ORIGIN US
SPEED ✓✓✓✓
INFO ✓✓✓✓
EASE ✓✓✓✓

Very strong on South Park, but other features
haven't hit the UK yet. The South Park pages offer
mini-clips and there are some excellent downloads
and games available. You can download bits of
Absolutely Fabulous too.

www.foxworld.com/simpsons
Home of the Simpsons

ORIGIN US
SPEED ✓✓✓✓
INFO ✓✓
VALUE ✓✓
EASE ✓✓✓✓

Visit Virtual Springfield, do the quiz, then visit
the shop – which seems to be the point of this
disappointing website. If you are a real fan then
go to www.snpp.com the Simpsons archive or
www.fandom.com/simpsons which is a little more
commercial but good nonetheless.

www.pythonline.com
Monty Python is not dead yet

ORIGIN UK
SPEED ✓✓✓✓
INFO ✓✓✓✓
VALUE ✓✓✓
EASE ✓✓✓✓

If you still hanker for Python humour, then there is a
corner of the internet set by just for you. It's still in
the process of being constructed but you can join the
Spam Club, buy merchandise, get news on the cast
or visit other Python fan sites.

www.theonion.com
AMERICA'S FINEST NEWS SOURCE

ORIGIN US	A great send-up of American tabloid newspapers,
SPEED ✓✓✓✓	this is one of the most visited sites on the internet
INFO ✓✓✓✓	and easily one of the funniest. For more satire try
EASE ✓✓✓✓	www.scoopthis.com.

www.comedy-zone.net
COMPLETE COMEDY GUIDE

ORIGIN UK	Excellent and wide-ranging comedy site with lots of
SPEED ✓✓✓	links and competitions, alongside quotes, jokes and
INFO ✓✓✓✓	chat.
EASE ✓✓✓	

www.losers.org
THE WEB'S LOSERS

ORIGIN US	A site that catalogues and rates the saddest sites
SPEED ✓✓✓	and sights on the web. One of the most fascinating
INFO ✓✓✓	giggles available, all web designers should see this.
EASE ✓✓✓✓	

Internet Service Provision

There are so many internet service providers (ISPs) that it would be impossible to review them all and it's moving so fast that any information we give may be outdated. Here are a few sites that will help you chose the right one for you.

www.net4nowt.com
THE PLACE TO START LOOKING FOR THE BEST ISP

ORIGIN UK	This is a directory of free internet service providers; it
SPEED ✓✓✓✓✓	gives news and advice on the best ones. There is a
INFO ✓✓✓✓✓	write-up on each ISP and it's usually very up-to-date
EASE ✓✓✓✓✓	with comments on costs and reliability. There is also a
	good summary table featuring all the ISPs that's useful
	for comparisons.

www.thematrix.org
INTERNET NEWS

ORIGIN UK
SPEED ✓✓✓✓
INFO ✓✓✓✓✓
EASE ✓✓✓✓✓

Find out what's really going on at this site, with features, a good archive and some competitions thrown in, they don't seem to miss much. See also **www.ispreview.co.uk** who also have an impressive site and are especially good at exposing fake ISPs.

Jewellery

see Fashion

Job Hunting

There are over 200 sites offering jobs or career advice but it's largely a matter of luck if you come across a job you like. Still it enables you to cover plenty of ground in a short space of time without trawling the newspapers. These sites offer the most options and best advice.

www.transdata-inter.co.uk/jobs-agencies/
TO CLARIFY AND SIMPLIFY ACCESS TO UK JOBS

ORIGIN UK
SPEED ✓✓✓
INFO ✓✓✓✓✓
EASE ✓✓✓✓✓

Don't let the long URL put you off, this is an excellent place to start on your search. The Directory lists all the major on-line employment agencies and ranks them: by the average number of vacancies, the regions they cover, whether they help and store CVs, and what industries they represent. Clicking on the name takes you right to the site you need.

www.careerguide.net
ON-LINE CAREER GUIDE

ORIGIN UK
SPEED ✓✓✓✓
INFO ✓✓✓✓✓
EASE ✓✓✓

This is a comprehensive service but with no career advice. There are many sections on job hunting, vacancies, CVs and professional institutions that can help.

www.careersolutions.co.uk
HELP TO GO FORWARD

ORIGIN UK
SPEED ✓✓✓
INFO ✓✓✓✓✓
EASE ✓✓✓✓

A good place to start if you're not sure what you want to do next in your career, or don't know where to start. Using the site enables you to narrow your options and clarify things. The most useful bit of the site is the list of links, which is laid out logically and is very helpful.

www.gisajob.co.uk
SEARCH FOR YOUR NEXT JOB HERE

ORIGIN UK
SPEED ✓✓✓✓
INFO ✓✓✓✓
EASE ✓✓✓✓✓

The largest of the on-line job sites with over 80,000 vacancies. You can search by description or sector and browse their top 100 jobs list. It's good for non-senior executive types.

www.stepstone.co.uk
EUROPEAN INTERNET RECRUITMENT

ORIGIN UK
SPEED ✓✓✓✓
INFO ✓✓✓✓
EASE ✓✓✓✓

The heavily advertised Stepstone has over 75,000 European vacancies and 14,000 in the UK. It's quick and easy-to-use and offers lots of time-saving cross-referencing. You can also register your CV. For other overseas jobs see **www.overseasjobs.com**.

www.i-resign.com/uk/
THE IN AND OUT OF RESIGNATION

ORIGIN US	Pay a visit before you send the letter, it offers a great
SPEED ✓✓✓	deal of advice both legal and sensible. The best
INFO ✓✓✓✓✓	section contains the funniest selection of resignation
EASE ✓✓✓	letters anywhere. There's also links to job finder sites
	and a CV writing service.

Legal Advice and the Law

We all need help with certain key events in life: marriages, moving house, making a will or even getting a divorce. Maybe you need advice on lesser issues like boundary disputes, problems with services or property? Here are several good sites that could really make a difference.

www.lawrights.co.uk
LEGAL INFORMATION AND SERVICES FOR ENGLAND AND WALES

ORIGIN UK	An extremely informative and useful site that covers
SPEED ✓✓✓	many aspects of the law in a clear and concise style.
INFO ✓✓✓✓✓	You can download some documents free or buy,
VALUE ✓✓✓✓	including case histories, news, tips and plenty of
EASE ✓✓✓✓	factsheets. See also **www.lawpack.co.uk** who offer
	legal documents
	such as wills, letting agreements and other contracts
	from £3.99.

www.uklegal.com
LEGAL RESOURCES AT YOUR FINGERTIPS

ORIGIN UK	This site offers a superb selection of links to
SPEED ✓✓✓✓	everything from private investigators to barristers
INFO ✓✓✓✓✓	to legal equipment suppliers.
EASE ✓✓✓✓	

www.desktoplawyer.net
THE UK'S FIRST ON-LINE LAWYER

ORIGIN UK
SPEED ✓✓✓✓
INFO ✓✓✓✓✓
VALUE ✓✓✓
EASE ✓✓✓✓

This site is quite easy-to-use if you know what you need and have read through the instructions carefully. First you register, then download the software (Rapidocs) that enables you to compile the document you need. The legal documents you create will cost from £5.99 upwards depending on complexity. You can call for advice or support as well, which costs around £1.75 a minute. The range of documents is huge and growing.

www.legal-aid.gov.uk
FOR HELP WITH LEGAL AID

ORIGIN UK
SPEED ✓✓✓✓
INFO ✓✓✓✓✓
EASE ✓✓

The official line on legal aid with guidance on how to use it, how to get information and news on latest changes to the legal aid scheme. It could be a lot more user friendly. For Scottish legal aid go to www.slab.org.uk.

www.terry.co.uk
ENGLISH LEGAL ADVICE

ORIGIN UK
SPEED ✓✓✓✓
INFO ✓✓✓✓✓
EASE ✓✓✓✓

The site of an English firm of solicitors that features a very good A–Z of legal terms, with clear, concise explanations in plain language.

www.wills-online.co.uk
HOW TO MAKE A WILL

ORIGIN UK
SPEED ✓✓✓
INFO ✓✓✓✓
VALUE ✓✓
EASE ✓✓✓✓

For just £35 for single or £49 for joint, you can fill out the on-line will form and wills-online will do the rest. They will also handle complex wills, but if yours is straight forward, then the service is quick and easy-to-use. www.makeyourwill.co.uk gives information on wills, and explains the process; you can start making a will on-line and they will complete it via the post, all for £58.75.

Magazines

www.britishmagazines.com
BRITISH MAGAZINES DIRECT

ORIGIN UK	Order just about any UK magazine and get it
SPEED ✓✓✓✓	delivered to your home free of charge. Its fast
INFO ✓✓✓✓	and easy-to-use, but you have to register. See also
VALUE ✓✓✓	www.whsmith.co.uk.
EASE ✓✓✓✓	

www.newsrack.com
JOHN MENZIES

ORIGIN UK	Search for the web site of the magazine or newspa-
SPEED ✓✓✓✓	per you want, then use the links. It covers most of
INFO ✓✓✓✓	the world, but you can't order from this site. For
EASE ✓✓✓✓	another site with masses of links to newspapers and
	magazines try www.actualidad.com.

Mobile phones

see Telecommunications

Motorcycles

see Transport

Movies

www.blackstar.co.uk
THE UK'S BIGGEST VIDEO STORE

ORIGIN UK
SPEED ✓✓✓✓
INFO ✓✓✓✓
VALUE ✓✓✓✓✓
EASE ✓✓✓✓

The biggest on-line video and DVD retailer, it claims to be able to get around 50,000 titles. Blackstar is very good value, boasts free delivery, and has a reputation for excellent customer service. If shopping around try **www.blockbuster.com**, who have different offers.

www.dvdstreet.infront.co.uk
FOR DVD ONLY

ORIGIN UK
SPEED ✓✓✓
INFO ✓✓✓✓
VALUE ✓✓✓✓
EASE ✓✓✓✓

Part of the Streets Online group, this is a great value and easy-to-use site that only sells DVD. Lots of other movie related features too such as the latest news and gossip or reviews. Delivery is free for the UK.

www.movietrak.com
RENT A DVD MOVIE

ORIGIN UK
SPEED ✓✓✓✓
INFO ✓✓✓✓
VALUE ✓✓✓✓
EASE ✓✓✓✓

The latest films are available to rent for £2.99 for 9 days. Pick the title of your choice and it's despatched the same day, you then return it 7 days later in the pre-paid envelope. The range offered is excellent covering ten major categories plus the latest releases, coming soon and a good search facility too.

www.reel.com
OVER 100,000 MOVIES

ORIGIN US
SPEED ✓✓✓✓
INFO ✓✓✓✓
VALUE ✓✓✓✓
EASE ✓✓✓✓

Here is a mixture of news, gossip, interviews, event listings and US-style outright selling. The content is excellent and you can get carried away browsing. The search facility is very good but shipping to the UK costs a minimum of $6. Watch out for local taxes and ensure that you can actually play the video in the UK. Also sells DVD and CDs.

http://uk.imdb.com
INTERNET MOVIE DATABASE

ORIGIN US	The best and most organised movie database on the
SPEED ✓✓✓	internet. It's very easy-to-use and every film buff's
INFO ✓✓✓✓✓	dream. In "What's Hot" check out the latest
EASE ✓✓✓✓	releases, get the latest movie news and reviews, do

the quizzes, leave a review or take up a recommendation. There's also a handy "if you liked then
you'll just love" section, and check out the stars'
birthdays. Another good database site is
www.allmovie.com, which has an excellent search
facility.

www.filmworld.co.uk
THE ONE STOP FILM SHOP

ORIGIN UK	Superb film buff's site. What makes this site stand
SPEED ✓✓✓	out is its very good search facility and the way it
INFO ✓✓✓✓✓	combines a great review site with an excellent shop.
VALUE ✓✓✓	The shop offers film memorabilia, finds "out of
EASE ✓✓✓✓	print" movies, and offers up to 25% off current

ones. Delivery is £1.

www.aint-it-cool-news.com
AIN'T IT JUST COOL

ORIGIN US	A renowned review site that can make or break
SPEED ✓✓✓	a movie in the US, it's very entertaining and
INFO ✓✓✓✓✓	endearing. Harry Knowles' movie reviews are by
EASE ✓✓✓✓	far the best bit of the site. You can search the

archive for a particular review or contribute a bit
of juicy gossip by e-mailing Harry direct. See also
www.moviecritic.com where you can rate movies
and review ratings. For a British angle, try
www.6degrees.co.uk which has reviews and a jobs
in the movies listing.

www.edrive.com
YOUR BACKSTAGE PASS

ORIGIN US
SPEED ✓✓✓
INFO ✓✓✓✓✓
EASE ✓✓✓✓

There are trendier sites than this, but it does have the latest gossip, news and views from Hollywood – and it's easier to use, and much more accessible than the others. See also **www.boxoff.com**, which is glitzier, but slower. If you've not had enough, go to **www.hollywood.com**, with over 1 million pages of information and trailers.

www.odeon.co.uk
BOOK YOUR TICKETS ON-LINE

ORIGIN UK
SPEED ✓✓✓
INFO ✓✓✓✓
VALUE ✓
EASE ✓✓✓✓

The Odeon's site is much like any other film sites in that you can buy films and see trailers and reviews, but you can also buy cinema tickets on-line. It may be slow at peak times. Booking fee is £2. You can also book tickets for Warner's cinemas and get the latest information at **www.warnervillage.co.uk**.

www.popcorn.co.uk
EVERYTHING FROM POSTERS TO WHAT'S ON WHERE

ORIGIN UK
SPEED ✓✓✓
INFO ✓✓✓✓✓
VALUE ✓✓
EASE ✓✓✓✓

Almost the complete package from Carlton TV, a great site for movie buffs as well as reliable local cinema listings complete with trailers giving you a taster before you put your coat on.

www.moviesounds.com
LISTEN TO YOUR FAVOURITE MOVIES

ORIGIN US
SPEED ✓✓
INFO ✓✓✓
EASE ✓✓✓

Download extracts from over 50 movies. It's a little confusing at first but once you've got the technology sorted out it's good fun.

Museums

see Art

Music

Before buying music or video on-line consider MP3. MP3 technology allows the compression of a music track into a file, which can be stored and played back. An MP3 player can be downloaded free on to your PC from several sites, the best being the original at www.mp3.com or the popular www.real.com and its RealPlayer. It can take about 40 minutes to download the player. You'll be able to listen to samples available in music stores and if you play CDs on your PC it will also record them. Once you've joined the MP3 revolution, there's an amazing amount of free music available, start at either web site where there are excellent search facilities. Other good MP3 players can be found at: www.winamp.com and www.sonique.com.

Other sites with lots of MP3 downloads and worth checking out are: www.songs.com, www.cductive.com, www.peoplesound.com, www.listen.com and www.liquidaudio.com (with liquidaudio player).

www.napster.com

THE NAPSTER MUSIC COMMUNITY

ORIGIN UK
SPEED ✓✓✓
INFO ✓✓✓✓
EASE ✓✓✓✓

Once you've downloaded Napster, you can locate and download your favourite music in MP3 format from one convenient, easy-to-use web site. This means that you can literally share the downloaded music of thousands of other MP3 fans. The legality of whether or not you can do this is under debate. Keep your eye on the press for further information.

www.clickmusic.co.uk

EVERYTHING YOU NEED TO KNOW ABOUT MUSIC

ORIGIN UK
SPEED ✓✓✓✓
INFO ✓✓✓✓
VALUE ✓✓✓✓
EASE ✓✓✓✓

This is a superb resource for all music fans. It offers quick access to details on a particular band, tickets, downloads, gigs or gossip. Shopping is straight forward using their Best 10 listings, just click on the store or use the search engine to find something specific.

www.dotmusic.com

ALL THE MUSIC NEWS

ORIGIN UK
SPEED ✓✓✓
INFO ✓✓✓✓
EASE ✓✓✓✓

Get the latest "insider" views from the music industry, with reviews, charts, chat and a good value on-line shop. These combined with first class design make this a great site.

www.jungle.com

JUNGLE MANIA!

ORIGIN UK
SPEED ✓✓✓✓
INFO ✓✓✓✓
VALUE ✓✓✓✓
EASE ✓✓✓✓

Jungle is easy, great fun to use and good value. There are four key areas:

- Jungle Beat, for all the latest in music and a comprehensive backlist. There's good information even on obscure albums.
- Jungle Vision for great offers on DVDs and videos.
- Jungle Play for masses of games for PCs and other formats.
- Jungle Computers for a wide selection of computers, software, hardware and consumables (discs, ink cartridges etc).

There is a loyalty scheme and delivery is free. Jungle also offers e-mail and an order tracking service.

www.hmv.co.uk
HIS MASTERS VOICE ON-LINE

ORIGIN UK
SPEED ✓✓✓
INFO ✓✓✓✓
VALUE ✓✓✓✓
EASE ✓✓✓✓

Very comprehensive with excellent features and offers on the latest CDs and videos. There are sections on most aspects of music as well as video, DVD and games with a good search facility. You can listen to selections from albums before buying if you have RealPlayer. Spoken word or books on tape are available as well.

www.virginmega.com
THE VIRGIN MEGA-STORE

ORIGIN UK
SPEED ✓✓
INFO ✓✓✓✓
VALUE ✓✓✓✓
EASE ✓✓✓✓

Loads of music categories means that you are spoilt for choice and you get good prices and free delivery. There is the usual search facility and a good deal of recommendation to help you. Become a Virgin V.I.P. and get special offers just for you. An interesting feature is the Virgin free radio. The site is a little slow.

www.cdnow.com
NOT JUST CDS

ORIGIN US
SPEED ✓✓✓
INFO ✓✓✓✓✓
VALUE ✓✓✓
EASE ✓✓✓✓

One of the original and easiest to use of the music sites, it has lots of features, such as downloads which enable you to sample albums for 30 days, a video section, and a recommendation service. Unfortunately UK residents can't take advantage of the excellent custom CD service.

www.cduniverse.com
FOR THE WIDEST RANGE AND GREAT OFFERS

ORIGIN US
SPEED ✓✓✓
INFO ✓✓✓✓
VALUE ✓✓✓✓✓
EASE ✓✓✓✓

Probably the site with the very best offers. There is a massive range to choose from and delivery normally takes only 5 days. You can also buy games, DVD and video. Excellent, but can be quite slow.

For more great offers on CDs try:
www.boxman.co.uk or **www.101cd.com**. It's as well
to check prices of CDs through price comparison
sites such as those listed on page 150.

www.minidiscnow.com

THE SOURCE FOR MINIDISCS

ORIGIN	US	
SPEED	✓✓✓	
INFO	✓✓✓	
VALUE	✓✓✓	
EASE	✓✓✓	

A fairly confusing site introducing the world of
minidiscs. It has a few bargains, but the emphasis is
on the latest technology so you have to hunt for
them. Also deals on CD players, digital cameras and
it's a good source for the latest gizmos from Japan.
Delivery to the UK varies.

www.ubl.com

THE ULTIMATE BAND LIST

ORIGIN	US	
SPEED	✓✓✓	
INFO	✓✓✓✓✓	
VALUE	✓✓✓	
EASE	✓✓✓✓	

It is the place for indulging in mountains of information on groups or singers. It has an excellent search
facility, and you can buy from the site as well,
although the prices are not as keen as elsewhere. For
a similar, probably better ordered experience try
www.allmusic.com, where you can also get excellent
information and videos.

www.classicalmusic.co.uk

EVERYTHING YOU NEED TO KNOW ABOUT
CLASSICAL MUSIC

ORIGIN	UK	
SPEED	✓✓✓✓	
INFO	✓✓✓✓	
VALUE	✓✓	
EASE	✓✓✓✓	

An excellent resource for devotees of classical music
with articles, guides, reviews and concert listings.
You can also buy CDs from the Global Music
Network who aren't the cheapest so it may pay to
buy elsewhere. For another very informative site
with an excellent selection of links try **www.classi-
cal.net** or for offers **www.mdcmusic.co.uk**.

www.operadata.co.uk
OPERA NOW MAGAZINE

ORIGIN UK
SPEED ✓✓✓✓
INFO ✓✓✓✓
VALUE ✓✓✓✓✓
EASE ✓✓✓✓

This site offers opera listings and provides background to the history of opera. To get the most out of it you have to subscribe to *Opera Now* magazine. For *Opera Magazine* go to www.opera.co.uk.

www.jazzonln.com
JAZZ ON-LINE

ORIGIN US
SPEED ✓✓✓✓
INFO ✓✓✓✓✓
EASE ✓✓✓✓

Whether you need help in working your way through the minefield that is jazz music, or you know what you want, Jazz On-line can provide it. Its accessible format covers all styles and it has a superb search facility. There is a lively debate section and you can ask Jazz Messenger just about anything. You can't buy from the site but it links to Amazon's music section. Try also **www.jazze.com** and **www.jazzcorner.com**.

www.bluesworld.com
HOMAGE TO THE BLUES

ORIGIN US
SPEED ✓✓✓✓
INFO ✓✓✓✓✓
VALUE ✓✓✓
EASE ✓✓✓✓

If you're into the blues then this is your kind of site. There are interviews, memorabilia, 78's auctions, bibliographies, discographies and lists of links to other blues sites. You can order CDs via Roots and Rhythm and if the mood takes you, order a guitar.

www.lyrics.com
THE WORDS TO HUNDREDS OF SONGS

ORIGIN US
SPEED ✓✓✓
INFO ✓✓✓
EASE ✓✓✓✓

There are songs from over 100 bands and artists including Oasis, Madonna, Britney Spears and Queen. You can also make requests and see if you know the words to any of the songs in the most wanted section. Don't expect to find any old favourites or classics though. For an alternative see **www.songfile.com** who offer a good selection of songs.

www.musicsearch.com

THE INTERNET'S MUSIC SEARCH ENGINE

ORIGIN US	Not that easy-to-use, but perseverance pays off
SPEED ✓✓✓	if you can't find that track or artist, or need infor-
INFO ✓✓✓✓	mation on a particular instrument or commercial
EASE ✓✓	aspect of music. There is a good facility to search
	the on-line stores for good deals or where to get the
	best range.

Concerts and tickets

www.liveconcerts.com

WELCOME TO THE CYBERCAST

ORIGIN US	Watch live concerts on-line! A great idea but let
SPEED ✓✓✓✓	down by "net congestion". You need Real Player to
INFO ✓✓✓	see the concerts and listen to the interviews and
VALUE ✓✓✓✓	recordings. It's very good for sampling different
EASE ✓✓✓	types of music and you can buy CDs as well.

www.bigmouth.co.uk

UK'S MOST COMPREHENSIVE GIG GUIDE

ORIGIN UK	UK based, with lots of links to band sites, news,
SPEED ✓✓✓	events listings and information on what's up and
INFO ✓✓✓✓	coming. Excellent search facilities and the ability to
VALUE ✓✓✓	buy tickets make this a very useful site for gig lovers
EASE ✓✓✓✓	everywhere. Oriented to Rock and Pop. For tour
	dates in the USA try **www.tourdates.com**.

www.ticketmaster.co.uk

TICKETS FOR EVERYTHING

ORIGIN UK
SPEED ✓✓✓✓
INFO ✓✓✓✓
VALUE ✓✓✓
EASE ✓✓✓

Book tickets for just about anything and you can run searches by venue, city or date. The site is split into four key sections:

- All Arts – theatre, classical, dance, comedy and events such as the Chelsea Flower show.
- All Concerts – gigs, jazz, clubs, rock and pop.
- All Family – shows, from Disney to air shows.
- All Sports – tickets for virtually every sporting occasion.

Nature and the Environment

www.panda.org

THE WORLD WIDE FUND FOR NATURE

ORIGIN UK
SPEED ✓✓✓✓
INFO ✓✓✓✓✓
EASE ✓✓✓✓

Called the WWF Global Network this is the official site for the WWF. Information on projects designed to save the world's endangered species by protecting their environment. You can: find out about the charity and how to contribute; visit the photo, video and art galleries; use the kid's section to teach children about wildlife.

An American organisation called the National Wildlife Fund has a similar excellent site at www.nwf.org.

www.nhm.ac.uk

THE NATURAL HISTORY MUSEUM

ORIGIN UK
SPEED ✓✓✓
INFO ✓✓✓✓
EASE ✓✓✓✓

A user friendly web site that covers everything from ants to eclipses. You can get the latest news, check out exhibitions, take a tour or watch the live antcast. Also details on the collections and contacts for answers to specific questions.

www.naturenet.net
COUNTRYSIDE, NATURE AND CONSERVATION

ORIGIN UK
SPEED ✓✓✓
INFO ✓✓✓✓✓
EASE ✓✓✓✓

Ignore the rather twee graphics and you'll find a great deal of information about nature in the UK. Their interests include: countryside law, upkeep of nature reserves, voluntary work, education and environmental news. You can also search the site for specifics and there is a good set of links to related sites. See also **www.wildlifetrust.org.uk**.

www.foe.co.uk
FRIENDS OF THE EARTH

ORIGIN UK
SPEED ✓✓✓✓
INFO ✓✓✓✓
EASE ✓✓✓✓

Not as worthy as you might imagine, this site offers a stack of information on food, pollution, green power, protecting wildlife in your area and the latest campaign news.

www.arkive.org.uk
ARCHIVE OF ENDANGERED SPECIES

ORIGIN UK
SPEED ✓✓✓
INFO ✓✓✓✓
EASE ✓✓✓

Sponsored by the Wildscreen Trust (**www.wildscreen.org.uk**) this site will eventually catalogue and picture all the world's endangered species. You can help by donating pictures and film.

www.envirolink.org
THE ON-LINE ENVIRONMENTAL COMMUNITY

ORIGIN US
SPEED ✓✓✓✓
INFO ✓✓✓✓✓
EASE ✓✓✓✓

A huge site focused on personal involvement in environment issues. There are over 25 sections with the key ones being: direct action, animal rights, what to boycott, a reference library, business and the environment, jobs and environmental events. There is also a good search facility on environment related topics.

For real campaigners go to the Greenpeace site **www.greenpeace.org** where you can find out about their latest activities and how to get involved.

www.planetdiary.com
A RECORD OF WHAT'S REALLY HAPPENING ON THE PLANET

ORIGIN US
SPEED ✓✓✓
INFO ✓✓✓✓✓
EASE ✓✓✓✓

Every week Planetdiary monitors and records world events in geological, astronomical, meteorological, biological and environmental terms and relays them back via this web site. It's done by showing an icon on a map of the world, which you then click on to find out more. Although very informative, a visit can leave you a little depressed.

www.coralcay.org
HOW YOU CAN JOIN IN

ORIGIN UK
SPEED ✓✓
INFO ✓✓✓✓
EASE ✓✓✓✓

In Coral Cay's words its aim is "providing resources to help sustain livelihoods and alleviate poverty through the protection, restoration and management of coral reefs and tropical forests". Sign up for an expedition or a science project in Honduras or the Philippines.

www.bbc.co.uk/nature
BBC WILDLIFE

ORIGIN UK
SPEED ✓✓✓
INFO ✓✓✓✓
VALUE ✓✓
EASE ✓✓✓✓

A brilliant nature offering from the BBC with sections on key wildlife programs and animal groups. The information is good and enhanced by view clips. Also visit **www.bbcwild.com**, the commercial site of the BBC wildlife unit with over 100,000 wildlife images available to buy. It's aimed at commercial organisations but plans to offer pictures for personal use at £15 each. It is a great place to browse for the remarkable images in the premium selection.

Needlework

see Hobbies

News and the Media

www.sky.co.uk/news

THE ULTIMATE NEWS SITE

ORIGIN UK	Sky News has fast developed a reputation for excel-
SPEED ✓✓✓	lence and that is reflected in their web site. It has the
INFO ✓✓✓✓✓	most rounded news service with good coverage
EASE ✓✓✓✓	across the world as well as the UK. You can view
	news clips or listen to news items or just browse the
	site, which also has sections on sport, business, tech-
	nology – even a few games.

www.bbc.co.uk/news

FROM THE BBC

ORIGIN UK	As you'd expect, the BBC site is excellent. It is simi-
SPEED ✓✓✓	lar to Sky without the adverts. You can also get the
INFO ✓✓✓✓✓	news in several languages, as well as tune in to the
EASE ✓✓✓✓	World Service or any of their radio stations.

www.itn.co.uk

INDEPENDENT TELEVISION NEWS

ORIGIN UK	A good site in that it doesn't bombard you with
SPEED ✓✓✓✓	everything at once, you get the main headline, and a
INFO ✓✓✓✓	sections listing for further information. See also
EASE ✓✓✓✓✓	www.teletext.co.uk who offer a similar site.

www.cnn.com
THE AMERICAN VIEW

ORIGIN US	CNN is superb on detail and breaking news with
SPEED ✓✓✓	masses of background information on each story.
INFO ✓✓✓✓✓	Has plenty of feature pieces too. However, the bias
VALUE ✓✓	is towards the American audience, for a similar
EASE ✓✓✓✓	service try **www.abcnews.com**.

www.ecola.com
NEWS DIRECTORY

ORIGIN US	A listing service that concentrates on news, it has
SPEED ✓✓✓	links to every major US news site, newspaper,
INFO ✓✓✓✓	magazines and resources such as a travel planner.
VALUE ✓✓	Also has excellent features on Europe.
EASE ✓✓✓✓	

www.drudgereport.com
NOW FOR THE REAL NEWS

ORIGIN US	One of the most visited sites on the web, it's a pain
SPEED ✓✓✓	to use, but the gossip and tips about upcoming
INFO ✓✓✓✓✓	features in the papers make it worthwhile. One of its
EASE ✓✓	best features is its superb set of links to other news
	sources.

www.foreignreport.com
PREDICT THE FUTURE

ORIGIN UK	The Foreign Report team attempt to pick out trends
SPEED ✓✓	and happenings that might lead to bigger interna-
INFO ✓✓✓✓	tional news events. Browsing through their track
EASE ✓✓✓	record shows they're pretty good at it too.

Office Supplies and Stationery

www.office-supplies.co.uk
OFFICE SUPPLIES ON-LINE

ORIGIN UK
SPEED ✓✓✓✓
INFO ✓✓✓✓
VALUE ✓✓✓
EASE ✓✓✓✓

Up to 14,000 items available, and if you place an order before 5.30 pm you get free next day delivery providing you spend over £35. It's really aimed at business users but if you need to buy a lot of stationery this is a good bet. See also www.harperoffice.co.uk and www.whsmith.co.uk.

Organiser and diary

www.organizer.com
ORGANISE YOURSELF

ORIGIN US
SPEED ✓✓
INFO ✓✓✓✓
EASE ✓✓✓✓

An American site that is just what it says it is, an organiser that allows you to list all your commitments and it will send e-mail reminders in good time. The UK version is due here soon.

www.opendiary.com
THE ON-LINE DIARY FOR THE WORLD

ORIGIN US
SPEED ✓✓✓
INFO ✓✓✓✓
EASE ✓✓✓

Your own personal organiser and diary, easy-to-use, genuinely helpful and totally anonymous. Simply register and away you go but follow the rules faithfully or you get deleted. Use it as you would any diary, go public or just browse other entries.

Organic

see Food and Drink

Over 50s

If you're over fifty then you are part of a group of people that many commentators think represent the greatest potential for use of the internet. If you're retired and you can afford a PC then there is a great deal to explore.

www.age-concern.org.uk
WORKING FOR ALL OLDER PEOPLE

ORIGIN UK	Learn how to get involved with helping older
SPEED ✓✓✓✓	people, get information and advice on all aspects on
INFO ✓✓✓✓✓	getting old and how to give a donation. There are
EASE ✓✓✓✓	also over 50 links to related and special interest
	sites.

www.idf50.co.uk
I DON'T FEEL FIFTY

ORIGIN UK	Graham Andrews is retired and this is his irreverent
SPEED ✓✓✓✓	magazine site. It's very positive about the power
INFO ✓✓✓✓✓	of being over 50, and it has a great deal of motiva-
EASE ✓✓✓	tional advice on how to get the best out of life,
	combined with a superb set of links to useful sites.

www.vavo.com
ON-LINE COMMUNITY

ORIGIN UK	This site is aimed at over 45s, but it offers a great
SPEED ✓✓✓✓	deal if you register, in terms of special deals on
INFO ✓✓✓✓	travel, health and financial advice, consumer tips,
EASE ✓✓✓	education and features on history and politics. An
	on-line shop is planned. There's also a great section
	on making retirement work for you.

Parenting

As a source of advice the internet has proved its worth and especially so for parents. As well as information, there are great shops and useful sites that filter out the worst of the web.

www.babyworld.co.uk

BE PART OF IT

ORIGIN UK
SPEED ✓✓✓
INFO ✓✓✓✓✓
VALUE ✓✓✓✓
EASE ✓✓✓✓

Babyworld is an on-line magazine that covers all aspects of parenthood, there's excellent advice on how to choose the right products for your baby and for the pregnancy itself. Its shop has everything you'd need at decent prices, delivery is £4.95 if you spend less than £75, free if you spend more.

www.webbaby.co.uk

FOR MOTHERS, FATHERS, BABIES AND BUMPS

ORIGIN UK
SPEED ✓✓✓✓
INFO ✓✓✓✓✓
VALUE ✓✓✓
EASE ✓✓✓✓

Excellent and wide-ranging magazine-style site with advice from conception to birth and beyond, there's also an on-line shop – Baby Boutique, a place to post your baby photos and a directory of relevant articles. You could also try **www.ukparents.co.uk** who offer a similar service but with more chat and better links.

www.babyzone.com

PARENTAL ADVICE

ORIGIN US
SPEED ✓✓✓✓
INFO ✓✓✓✓✓
EASE ✓✓✓

This massive, comprehensive, American site on parenting gives a week-by-week account of pregnancy, information on birth and early childhood. The shop is not open to UK residents.

www.families.co.uk
FAMILY WEB GUIDE

ORIGIN UK
SPEED ✓✓✓✓
INFO ✓✓✓
VALUE ✓✓✓
EASE ✓✓✓✓

A mass of information and links for all the family, from books to holidays to child-friendly pubs, it's excellent if you want to plan outings or a break for the family. Check out **www.parentsoup.com** who offer information on a wide range of topics.

www.babydirectory.com
A-Z OF BEING A PARENT

ORIGIN UK
SPEED ✓✓✓
INFO ✓✓✓
EASE ✓✓✓✓

The Baby Directory catalogue is relevant to most parts of the UK. It lists local facilities and amenities to care for and occupy your child. The quality of information varies by area.

www.babyweb.co.uk
BABY PICTURES

ORIGIN UK
SPEED ✓✓✓
INFO ✓✓✓
EASE ✓✓✓

If you want to have a picture of your new arrival with all the birth details highlighted on the web here's where to go!

www.bloomingmarvellous.co.uk
MATERNITY, NURSERY AND BABY WEAR

ORIGIN UK
SPEED ✓✓✓✓
INFO ✓✓✓
VALUE ✓✓✓
EASE ✓✓✓✓

Excellent on-line store with 30 or so lines available to buy, or you can order the catalogue. Delivery in the UK is £3.95.

www.cyberpatrol.com
INTERNET FILTERING SOFTWARE

ORIGIN US
SPEED ✓✓✓
INFO ✓✓✓✓
VALUE ✓✓✓
EASE ✓✓✓✓

The best for filtering out unwanted web sites, images and words. As with all similar programs, it quickly becomes outdated but will continue to weed out the worst. You can download a free trial from the site. See also **www.netnanny.com**, whose site offers more advice and seems to be updated more regularly.

www.pin-parents.com
PARENTS INFORMATION NETWORK

ORIGIN US	Provides good advice for parents worried about
SPEED ✓✓✓✓	children using computers. It has links to support
INFO ✓✓✓✓✓	sites, guidance on how to surf the net, evaluations
VALUE ✓✓✓	of software and buyer's guides to PCs.
EASE ✓✓✓✓	

www.teenadviceonline.com
SOLVING TEENAGE ANGST

ORIGIN US	If you have a problem with your teenager, then a
SPEED ✓✓✓	stop here might just save a great deal of time and
INFO ✓✓✓✓✓	worry for you and for them. TAO have a good track
EASE ✓✓✓	record; they have adult and teenage counsellors.

Pets

Pet web sites and on-line pet shops were one of the biggest growth areas in 1999. Some of the sites are very well designed and other retailers should take note.

www.pets-pyjamas.co.uk
THE COMPLETE PETS WEB SITE

ORIGIN UK	Go to Petmags for comprehensive news and infor-
SPEED ✓✓✓	mation, take part in on-line discussions, chat in
INFO ✓✓✓✓	Petpals, do a competition or quiz in Petfun, even set
VALUE ✓✓✓	up a website for your pet. The most important
EASE ✓✓✓✓	section is Petshops consisting of PetsPyjamas' own

shop plus links to a bookshop with over 1000 titles and **www.animail.co.uk** a more general value led pet shop. For another good on-line pet store visit www.petplanet.co.uk or www.petlink.co.uk who have an excellent links to other pet sites.

www.dogsonline.co.uk
DOGS, DOGS AND MORE DOGS

ORIGIN UK
SPEED ✓✓✓
INFO ✓✓✓✓✓
VALUE ✓✓
EASE ✓✓✓✓

All you'd ever want from a web site about dogs. There's information on breeding, where to get dogs, events, directories, how to find hotels that accept dogs, classified ads and insurance.

For more information on dogs try www.canismajor.com an American magazine site, the comprehensive www.canineworld.com or www.the-kennel-club.org.uk for the official line on dogs and breeding with information on Crufts and links to related web sites.

www.ncdl.org.uk
NATIONAL CANINE DEFENCE LEAGUE

ORIGIN UK
SPEED ✓✓
INFO ✓✓✓✓✓
VALUE ✓✓✓
EASE ✓✓✓✓

Excellent web site featuring the charitable works of the NCDL the largest charity of its type. Get advice on how to adopt a dog, tips on looking after one and download a doggie screensaver. For Battersea Dogs Home go to www.dogshome.org who have a well-designed site.

www.cats.org.uk
HOME OF CAT PROTECTION

ORIGIN UK
SPEED ✓✓✓
INFO ✓✓✓✓
VALUE ✓✓✓
EASE ✓✓✓✓

A well-designed and informative site, with information on caring, re-homing, news and general advice, there's even a section for children called the Kitten club and an archive of cat photos. There's also an on-line shop that offers free delivery in the UK. For more information and links on cats go to www.moggies.co.uk.

www.equiworld.net
GLOBAL EQUINE INFORMATION

ORIGIN UK
SPEED ✓✓✓
INFO ✓✓✓✓✓
EASE ✓✓✓✓

A directory, magazine and advice centre in one with incredible detail plus some fun stuff too. The shop is basically links to specialist traders. For health advice go to www.horseadvice.com. Also the comprehensive www.equine-world.co.uk.

www.pethealthcare.co.uk
PET INSURANCE

ORIGIN UK
SPEED ✓✓✓✓
INFO ✓✓✓
VALUE ✓✓✓
EASE ✓✓✓✓

To insure your pet to cover vet's bill, then here's a good place to start. For other comparable quotes try www.healthy-pets.co.uk.

www.giveusahome.co.uk
RE-HOMING A PET

ORIGIN UK
SPEED ✓✓✓
INFO ✓✓✓✓✓
EASE ✓✓✓

A nice idea, a web site devoted to helping you save animals that need to be re-homed, it's got a large amount of information by region on shelters, vets and the animals themselves as well as an entertaining cartoon for kids.

Photography

www.rps.org
THE ROYAL PHOTOGRAPHIC SOCIETY

ORIGIN UK
SPEED ✓✓✓
INFO ✓✓
EASE ✓✓✓

A worthy, dull site dedicated to the works of the RPS; you can get details of the latest exhibitions, become a member, get the latest news about the world of photography. Good for links to other related sites. Sadly there aren't many pictures, which is an opportunity missed.

www.nmpft.org.uk
NATIONAL MUSEUM OF PHOTOGRAPHY, FILM AND TELEVISION

ORIGIN UK
SPEED ✓✓✓
INFO ✓✓✓✓
EASE ✓✓✓✓

Details of this Bradford museum via a high tech website, opening times and directions, what's on, education resources and a very good museum guide. Some pages are still under construction.

www.eastman.org
THE INTERNATIONAL MUSEUM OF PHOTOGRAPHY

ORIGIN US
SPEED ✓✓✓
INFO ✓✓✓✓
EASE ✓✓✓✓

George Eastman founded Kodak and this New York-based museum too. This site is comprehensive and amongst other things you can learn about the history of photography, visit the photographic and film galleries, or obtain technical information. Become a member which entitles you to benefits such as free admission and copies of their *Image* magazine.

www.nationalgeographic.com/photography
HOME OF THE NATIONAL GEOGRAPHIC MAGAZINE

ORIGIN US
SPEED ✓✓✓✓
INFO ✓✓✓✓✓
EASE ✓✓✓

Synonymous with great photography, this excellent site offers much more. There are sections on travel, exhibitions, maps, news, education, and for kids. In the photography section pick up tips and techniques, follow their photographers various locations, read superb articles and accompanying shots in the Visions Galleries. Good links to other photographic sites.

www.pathfinder.com/Life/
LIFE MAGAZINE

ORIGIN US
SPEED ✓✓✓
INFO ✓✓✓✓
VALUE ✓✓
EASE ✓✓

Life Magazine, is wonderfully nostalgic and still going strong. There are several sections, features with great photos, excellent articles, and an option to subscribe; however they could do more and it's frustrating to use.

www.corbis.com
THE PLACE FOR PICTURES ON THE INTERNET

ORIGIN US
SPEED ✓✓✓
INFO ✓✓✓✓✓
VALUE ✓✓✓
EASE ✓✓✓✓

Another Microsoft product, this is probably the world's largest on-line picture library. Use the pictures to enhance presentations, web site, screen-savers, or to make e-cards for friends. You can also buy pictures framed or unframed which are good value, but shipping to the UK can be expensive.

www.bjphoto.co.uk
THE BRITISH JOURNAL OF PHOTOGRAPHY

ORIGIN UK
SPEED ✓✓✓
INFO ✓✓✓
EASE ✓✓✓✓

For magazine-type material on photography. Access their archive of articles or visit picture galleries that contain work from contemporary photographers; find out about careers in photography and where to buy the best photographic gear.

www.whichcamera.co.uk
FIND THE RIGHT CAMERA

ORIGIN UK
SPEED ✓✓
INFO ✓✓✓✓✓
EASE ✓✓

Get advice on the best camera for you then use links to find your local dealer or to the manufacturer direct. The information is very good, but the site can be very slow and the graphics are irritating.

www.euro-foto.com
THE PHOTO SUPERSTORE

ORIGIN UK	This company offer a massive range of photographic
SPEED ✓✓✓	and related products. It has a good search facility
INFO ✓✓✓✓	which is easier to use than browsing through the site.
VALUE ✓✓✓✓	There are also some good offers and free delivery
EASE ✓✓✓	is available although currently as part of a sales
	promotion.

Price Checkers

There are many books, music and video price comparison sites; one of the best is at www.shopsmart.co.uk; however, the sites listed here allow you to check the prices for on-line stores across a much wider range of merchandise.

www.checkaprice.com
CONSTANTLY CHECKING PRICES

ORIGIN UK	Compare prices across nearly sixty different product
SPEED ✓✓✓	types, from the usual books to cars, holidays, mort-
INFO ✓✓✓✓	gages and electrical goods. If it can't do it for you, it
VALUE ✓✓✓✓✓	patches you through to a site that can.
EASE ✓✓✓✓	

www.shopgenie.co.uk
COMPARES PRICES IN REAL TIME

ORIGIN UK	Claims to be the most up to date in catching the
SPEED ✓✓✓	prices for books, music, video, games, computer
INFO ✓✓✓✓	hardware and software. You could also try
VALUE ✓✓✓✓	**www.price-search.net** who cover computers and
EASE ✓✓✓	electrical goods as well, as do **www.pricewatch.com**.

Property

Every Estate Agent worth their salt has got a web site, and in theory finding the house of your dreams has never been easier. These sites have been designed to help you through the real life minefield.

www.upmystreet.com
FIND OUT ABOUT WHERE YOU WANT TO GO

ORIGIN UK
SPEED ✓✓✓
INFO ✓✓✓✓✓
EASE ✓✓✓

Type in the postcode and up pops almost every statistic you need to know about the area in question. Spooky, but fascinating, it's a good guide featuring not only house prices, but also schools, the local MP, local authority information, crime and links to services.

www.propertyfinder.co.uk
UK'S BIGGEST PROPERTY DATABASE

ORIGIN UK
SPEED ✓✓✓✓
INFO ✓✓✓✓
EASE ✓✓✓✓

With over 20,000 properties available, this is a good place to start looking, it's quick to use and there is usually detailed information on each property with links to participating estate agents.

www.reallymoving.com
MAKING MOVING EASIER

ORIGIN UK
SPEED ✓✓✓
INFO ✓✓✓✓✓
EASE ✓✓✓

A directory of sites and help for home buyers including mortgages, removal firms, surveyors, solicitors, van hire and home improvements. You can get on-line quotes on some services and there's good regional information. The property search is fast and has plenty to choose from.

www.ihavemoved.com
MOVING HELP

ORIGIN UK
SPEED ✓✓✓
INFO ✓✓✓✓✓
EASE ✓✓✓✓✓

A confidential service that you can use to inform everyone that matters that you have moved house, if nothing else it's a great checklist.

www.property-sight.co.uk
MADE TO MEASURE

ORIGIN UK
SPEED ✓✓✓
INFO ✓✓✓✓
EASE ✓✓✓

One of the best for house purchases in the UK, the site is up to date and easy-to-use, with around 8000 registered properties. Use the detailed search facility and register your requirements.

www.cyberhomes.co.uk
RENT, LEASE OR BUY

ORIGIN UK
SPEED ✓✓✓
INFO ✓✓✓
EASE ✓✓✓

Plenty of properties to lease or rent here, also homes for sale and a good estate agent database. It's quick but a little confusing to use. See also www.homelet.co.uk who claim to take the risk out of renting by offering sound advice and insurance.

www.propertylive.co.uk
TAKE THE PAIN OUT OF MOVING HOUSE

ORIGIN UK
SPEED ✓✓✓✓
INFO ✓✓✓✓
EASE ✓✓✓

Plenty of advice on moving from the National Association of Estate Agents, plus lists of properties for sale. There is a quick search facility, although fewer properties than some sites, it's worth a visit.

www.freehomeindex.com
ADVERTISE YOUR PROPERTY FOR FREE

ORIGIN UK
SPEED ✓✓
INFO ✓✓✓✓
EASE ✓✓✓

As well as free advertising, get mortgage and insurance advice, area information and browse the houses for sale. The site is a little slow, and the

search facility could be much better.
For more properties try these sites:
www.houseweb.co.uk
www.easier.co.uk
www.homefreehome.co.uk
www.heritage.co.uk – listed buildings specialists.

www.french-property.com
No. 1 for France

ORIGIN UK	If you are fed up with the UK and want to move to
SPEED ✓✓✓✓	France this is the site to start with, they offer prop-
INFO ✓✓✓✓	erties for rent or for sale in all regions and can link
EASE ✓✓✓	you with other estate agents.

Quizzes

see Games

Radio

You need a decent downloadable player such as RealPlayer (www.real.com) or Windows media player before you start listening. RealPlayer in particular gives you access to many stations and allows you to add more. The downside is that quality is sometimes affected by "net congestion".

www.bbc.co.uk/radio
The best of the BBC

ORIGIN UK	Listen to the news and the latest hits while you
SPEED ✓✓✓✓	work, just select the station you want. There's also a
INFO ✓✓✓✓✓	great deal of information on each major station, as
EASE ✓✓✓✓	well as a comprehensive listing service. Some
	features will be missing due to rights issues. Works
	on RealPlayer.

www.virginradio.com

VIRGIN ON AIR

ORIGIN UK
SPEED ✓✓
INFO ✓✓✓✓✓
EASE ✓✓✓✓

Excellent web site with plenty of information about the station, its schedule and stars. There's also the latest music news. The site has an annoying amount of advertising though. You can listen if you have Quicktime, Windows Media or RealPlayer.

Other independent radio stations on-line are:
www.classicfm.com – using Windows Media player
www.jazzfm.com – using Windows Media player
www.galaxy-radio.co.uk – using Windows Media player
www.capitalfm.com – using RealPlayer
www.coolfm.co.uk – using RealPlayer
www.heart1062.co.uk – using Windows Media player
www.lbc.co.uk – using Real Audio.

www.radioacademy.org

UK'S GATEWAY TO RADIO

ORIGIN UK
SPEED ✓✓✓✓
INFO ✓✓✓✓✓
EASE ✓✓✓✓

Radio Academy is a charity that covers all things to do with radio including news, events and its advancement in education and information. It has a list of all UK stations including those that offer web casts. For a massive list of stations go to Yahoo's **www.broadcast.com/radio**.

www.netradio.net

RADIO TAILORED FOR YOU

ORIGIN US
SPEED ✓✓✓✓
INFO ✓✓✓✓✓
VALUE ✓✓✓
EASE ✓✓✓✓✓

Pick any one of its specialist 120 channels; tune in using RealPlayer or Windows, and if you like the track you can also buy the album. A specialist has programmed each channel to play a type of music and the selection is consistently good. A site with a real "wow factor". Other good radio sites are

www.comfm.fr a French site with access to almost 3500 live stations and the American **www.webradio.com**.

Reference and Encyclopaedia Sites

If you are stuck with your homework or want an answer to any question, then this is where the internet really comes into its own. With these sites you are bound to find what you are looking for.

www.refdesk.com

THE BEST SINGLE SOURCE FOR FACTS

ORIGIN US
SPEED ✓✓✓
INFO ✓✓✓✓✓
EASE ✓✓✓✓

Singled out for its sheer size and scope, this site offers information and links to just about anything, its mission is "only about indexing quality internet sites and assisting visitors in navigating these sites". It's won numerous awards and it never fails to impress.

www.about.com

IT'S ABOUT INFORMATION

ORIGIN UK
SPEED ✓✓✓
INFO ✓✓✓✓✓
EASE ✓✓✓✓✓

A superb resource, easy-to-use and great for beginners learning to search for information. Experts help you to find what you need every step of the way. It offers information on a wide range of topics from the arts and sciences to shopping. Also worth a visit is **www.libraryspot.com**, which is similar in scope but has a more literary emphasis.

www.ipl.org
THE INTERNET PUBLIC LIBRARY

ORIGIN US
SPEED ✓✓✓
INFO ✓✓✓✓✓
EASE ✓✓✓

Another excellent resource, there are articles on a vast range of subjects concentrating on literary criticism. Almost every country and literature is covered. If there isn't anything at the library, there is invariably a link to take you to an alternative web site.

www.homeworkelephant.free-online.co.uk
LET THE ELEPHANT HELP WITH HOMEWORK

ORIGIN UK
SPEED ✓✓✓
INFO ✓✓✓✓✓
EASE ✓✓✓✓

A resource with some 700 links aimed at helping students achieve great results, there's help with specific subjects, hints & tips, help for parents and teachers. It's constantly being updated, so worth checking regularly.

www.maths-help.co.uk
E-MAIL YOUR MATHS PROBLEMS

ORIGIN UK
SPEED ✓✓✓
INFO ✓✓✓✓✓
EASE ✓✓✓✓✓

Send your queries to maths-help and they'll e-mail you back the answers in a couple of days. You can also visit the knowledge bank to see past queries and answers.

www.pinchbeck.com
ANSWERS TO HOMEWORK, FREE

ORIGIN US
SPEED ✓✓✓
INFO ✓✓✓✓✓
EASE ✓✓✓

This huge database is one of the biggest on-line resources of its type, with some 600 links to a variety of reference sites. Homework was never so easy; however, to British eyes, it can be quite irritating in style. For more homework links see **www.schoolwork.org** and the wide-ranging **www.studyweb.com** with over 118,000 URLs listed.

www.eserver.org
THE ENGLISH SERVER

ORIGIN US
SPEED ✓✓✓
INFO ✓✓✓✓✓
EASE ✓✓✓

A rather dry humanities site, however it provides a vast amount of resource data about almost every cultural topic. There are some 20,000 texts, articles and essays available.

http://classics.mit.edu
THE INTERNET CLASSICS ARCHIVE

ORIGIN US
SPEED ✓✓✓✓
INFO ✓✓✓✓✓
EASE ✓✓✓✓

An excellent site for researching into the classics, it's easy-to-use and fast, with more than enough information for homework whatever the level.

www.omsakthi.org/religions.html
INFORMATION ON ALL THE WORLD'S RELIGIONS

ORIGIN US
SPEED ✓✓✓
INFO ✓✓✓✓✓
EASE ✓✓✓

This site provides a clear description of each religion including values and basic beliefs, with links to books on each one.

www.ntu.edu.sg/library/stat/statdata.htm
STATISTICS AND MORE STATISTICS

ORIGIN SINGAPORE
SPEED ✓✓✓✓
INFO ✓✓✓✓✓
EASE ✓✓✓

Free information and statistics about every world economy, not that easy to use at first, but it's all there. For the UK go to the source of the statistics at www.statitistics.gov.uk.

www.atlapedia.com
THE WORLD IN BOTH PICTURES AND NUMBERS

ORIGIN US
SPEED ✓✓✓
INFO ✓✓✓✓✓
EASE ✓✓✓

Contains full colour political and physical maps of the world with statistics and very detailed information on each country. It can be very slow, so you need patience, but the end results are worth it.

www.dk.com
DORLING KINDERSLEY PUBLISHING

ORIGIN UK
SPEED ✓✓✓
INFO ✓✓✓✓✓
EASE ✓✓✓

Offers on DK books and free delivery is reason enough to visit this site, but you can also get access to the Eyewitness reference series offering 2 million words and 40,000 pictures.

Encyclopaedias and Dictionaries

http://encarta.msn.com
THE ENCARTA ENCYCLOPAEDIA

ORIGIN US
SPEED ✓✓✓✓
INFO ✓✓✓✓✓
EASE ✓✓✓✓

Even though the complete thing is only available to buy, there is access to over 16,000 articles and reference notes via the concise version. It's fast and easy-to-use. If you can't find what you're looking for here, then go to www.encyclopedia.com or www.eb.com, home of the Encyclopaedia Britannica for which you need to either register or subscribe.

Using the WH Smith ISP www.whsmith.co.uk you get free access to the Hutchinson Family encyclopaedia, which has 18,000 entries and is good for GCSE and National Curriculum studies. You can get a 14-day free trial at the site.

For children, good alternative encyclopaedias can be found at Dr Universe www.wsu.edu/DrUniverse/ and at www.letsfindout.com, home of the Knowledge Adventure encyclopedia.

www.thesaurus.com
IF YOU CAN'T FIND THE WORD

ORIGIN US
SPEED ✓✓✓
INFO ✓✓✓✓✓
EASE ✓✓✓✓

Based on Roget's Thesaurus this site will enable you to find alternative words, useful but not worth turning your PC on in place of the book. For the equivalent dictionary site, go to www.dictionary.com; you can play word games as an added feature on both sites.

For a dictionary that specialises in jargon and internet terms only go to www.jargon.net or www.netdictionary.com for enlightenment.

While www.onelook.com claim to offer access to almost 600 dictionaries and nearly 3 million words, at a fast and easy-to-use site, it also offers a price checking service for on-line shopping.

http://dictionaries.travlang.com
FOREIGN LANGUAGE DICTIONARIES

ORIGIN US
SPEED ✓✓✓✓
INFO ✓✓✓✓✓
EASE ✓✓✓✓✓

There are 16 language dictionaries on this site, just select the dictionary you want, then type in the word or sentence to be translated – it couldn't be simpler. Originally aimed at the traveller, but it's very useful in this context.

Science and Space

The internet was originally created by a group of scientists who wanted to faster, more efficient communication and today, scientists around the world use the net to compare data and collaborate. In addition, the layman has access to the wonders of science in a way that's never been possible before, and as for homework – well now it's a doddle.

www.sciseek.com
ON-LINE RESOURCE FOR SCIENCE AND NATURE

ORIGIN US
SPEED ✓✓✓
INFO ✓✓✓✓
EASE ✓✓✓

A good place to start, Sciseek lists over 1000 sites on everything from agriculture to chemistry to health to physics, each site is reviewed and you have the opportunity to leave comments too.

www.sciencemuseum.org.uk
THE SCIENCE MUSEUM

ORIGIN UK
SPEED ✓✓✓
INFO ✓✓✓✓
EASE ✓✓✓✓

An excellent site detailing the major attractions at the museum with 3D graphics and features on exhibitions and forthcoming events. See also www.exploratorium.edu, a similar site by an American museum.

www.madsci.org
THE LAB THAT NEVER SLEEPS

ORIGIN US
SPEED ✓✓✓
INFO ✓✓✓✓
EASE ✓✓✓

A site that successfully combines science with fun, you can ask a question of a mad scientist, browse the links list or check out the archives in the library.

www.howstuffworks.com
HOW STUFF REALLY WORKS

ORIGIN US
SPEED ✓✓✓✓
INFO ✓✓✓✓✓
EASE ✓✓✓✓✓

A popular site, for nerds and kids young and old; it's easy-to-use and fascinating. There are 27 sections ranging from the obvious engines and technology, through to food and the weather. The current top 10 section, features the latest answers to the questions of the day. It's written in a very concise, clear style with lots of cross-referencing.

www.hotbox.co.uk
GADGETS GALORE

ORIGIN UK
SPEED ✓✓✓
INFO ✓✓✓✓
VALUE ✓✓✓
EASE ✓✓✓

Impress your friends with your knowledge of the newest gadgets, innovations or what's likely to be the next big thing. You can also show off even more by buying them at the on-line shop, which is good value when you take into account the free delivery.

www.newscientist.com
NEW SCIENTIST MAGAZINE

ORIGIN UK
SPEED ✓✓✓
INFO ✓✓✓✓✓
EASE ✓✓✓✓

Much better than the usual on-line magazines because of its creative use of archive material which is simultaneously fun and serious. It's easy to search the site or browse through back features – the Even More Bizarre bit is particularly entertaining. For a more traditional science magazine site go to Popular Science at **www.popsci.com**, great for information on the latest gadgets.

www.discovery.com
THE DISCOVERY CHANNEL

ORIGIN UK
SPEED ✓✓
INFO ✓✓✓✓✓
EASE ✓✓✓✓

A superb site for science and nature lovers, it's inspiring as well as educational. Order the weekly newsletter, get information on discoveries plus features on pets, space, travel, lifestyle and school.

Space

www.space.com
MAKING SPACE POPULAR

ORIGIN US
SPEED ✓✓
INFO ✓✓✓✓✓
VALUE ✓✓
EASE ✓✓✓

An education-oriented site dedicated to space; there's news, mission reports, technology, history, personalities, a kid's section and plenty of pictures. The science section explores the planets and earth. You can buy goods at the space shop with delivery charge dependent on purchase.

www.seds.org/billa/tnp
THE NINE PLANETS

ORIGIN US
SPEED ✓✓✓
INFO ✓✓✓✓✓
EASE ✓✓✓✓

A multi-media tour of the nine planets, stunning photography and interesting facts combined with good text.

www.nasa.gov
THE OFFICIAL NASA SITE

ORIGIN US
SPEED ✓✓✓
INFO ✓✓✓✓✓
EASE ✓✓✓

This huge site provides comprehensive information on the US National Aeronautical and Space Administration. There are details on each NASA site, launch timings, sections for news, kids, project updates, and links to their specialist sites such the Hubble space telescope, Mars and Earth observation. For Britain's place in space go to www.bnsc.gov.uk.

www.nauts.com
THE ASTRONAUT CONNECTION

ORIGIN US
SPEED ✓✓✓
INFO ✓✓✓✓✓
EASE ✓✓✓

In their words, "The Astronaut Connection has worked to create an educational and entertaining resource for space enthusiasts, young and old, to learn about astronauts and space exploration". And that just about sums up this excellent and informative site.

www.astronomynow.com
THE UK'S BEST SELLING ASTRONOMY MAG

ORIGIN UK
SPEED ✓✓
INFO ✓✓✓✓
VALUE ✓✓
EASE ✓✓✓

Get the news and views from a British angle, plus reviews on the latest books. The store basically offers back issues of the magazine and posters.

www.setiathome.ssl.berkeley.edu/
GET IN TOUCH WITH AN ALIEN

ORIGIN UK
SPEED ✓✓✓
INFO ✓✓✓✓
EASE ✓✓✓

To borrow the official site description 'SETI@home is a scientific experiment that uses internet-connected computers in the Search for Extraterrestrial Intelligence (SETI). You can participate by running a free program that downloads and analyses radio telescope data. You could be the first!

Shoes

see Fashion

Search Engines

The best way to find what you want from the internet is to use a search engine. Even the best only cover at most 50% of the available web sites; so if you can't find what you want from one, try another. These are the best and most user friendly.

http://uk.yahoo.com
FOR THE UK AND IRELAND

ORIGIN US	The UK arm of Yahoo! is the biggest and one of the
SPEED ✓✓✓✓	most established search engines. It's now much more
INFO ✓✓✓✓✓	than just a search facility as it offers a huge array of
EASE ✓✓✓	other services: from news to finance to shopping to
	sport to travel to games. You can restrict your
	search to just UK or Irish sites.

www.mirago.co.uk
THE UK SEARCH ENGINE

ORIGIN UK	Mirago searches the whole web but prioritises the
SPEED ✓✓✓✓	search for UK families and businesses. It's very
INFO ✓✓✓✓✓	quick, easy-to-use and offers many of the services
EASE ✓✓✓✓✓	you get from Yahoo! You can tailor your search very
	easily to exclude stuff you won't need. For another
	UK oriented site try **www.ukplus.co.uk**.

www.ask.co.uk
ASK JEEVES

ORIGIN US	Just type in your question and the famous old butler
SPEED ✓✓✓✓	will come back with the answer. It may be a
INFO ✓✓✓✓	bit gimmicky but works very well, it's great for
EASE ✓✓✓✓✓	beginners and reliable for old hands too.

www.mamma.com
THE MOTHER OF ALL SEARCH ENGINES

ORIGIN US
SPEED ✓✓✓✓
INFO ✓✓✓✓
EASE ✓✓✓✓

Mamma claim to have technology enabling them to search the search engines thoroughly and get the most pertinent results to your query – it's fast too, your query comes back with the answer and the search engine it came from.

www.google.com
BRINGING ORDER TO THE WEB

ORIGIN US
SPEED ✓✓✓✓✓
INFO ✓✓✓
EASE ✓✓✓✓✓

Google is all about speed and accuracy. Using a complicated set of rules they claim to be able to give the most relevant results in the quickest time, in fact they even tell you how fast they are. It's easier to use than most, but seems to cover less than Mamma and Yahoo!

Finding the search engine that suits you is a matter of personal requirements and taste, here are some other very good, tried and trusted ones: www.altavista.com, www.excite.co.uk, www.lycos.co.uk, www.infoplease.com, www.hotbot.com, www.msn.co.uk.

www.searchenginewatch.com
MONITORING THE SEARCH ENGINES

ORIGIN US
SPEED ✓✓✓
INFO ✓✓✓✓✓
EASE ✓✓✓

Reviews all the many search engines and gives tips on how to get the best out of them, there's also a free newsletter to keep you really up to speed.

Skiing

see Sport

Shopping

To many people shopping is what the internet is all about, and although it's not really taken off for high priced goods, it does offer an opportunity to get some tremendous bargains. Watch out for hidden costs such as delivery charges or finance deals that seem attractive until you compare them with what's available elsewhere. For help on finding comparative prices, see the Price Checkers entry on page 150.

One of the best places to start is at the Which? Magazine web site, www.which.net, who run a scheme to protect on-line shoppers. They sign up retailers to a code of practice that covers the way they trade.

To quote Which?:

"The Which Web Trader Scheme is designed to make sure consumers get a fair deal and to provide them with protection if things go wrong. Which? Web Traders agree to meet and abide by our Code of Practice. If we receive complaints from consumers about the service from a web trader displaying the Which Web Trader logo, we will investigate and may withdraw our permission for a trader to display the logo."

Sites listed in the guide which are part of the scheme and follow the code of practice are flagged with this symbol – **W?WT** . *You can get a complete list from the Which? web site.*

The mainstays of the high street

www.marks-and-spencer.co.uk

THIS ATTRACTIVE SITE OFFERS A NUMBER OF OPTIONS SOME 200 LINES AVAILABLE TO BUY:

ORIGIN UK	1. Home – with lots of ideas. Register for the catalogue or wedding service.
SPEED ✓✓	
INFO ✓✓✓✓	2. Fashion – window shop the current range.
VALUE ✓✓✓	
EASE ✓✓✓✓	3. Food – recipes, tips and food news.

4. Financial – take advantage of their financial services.
5. The Store – buy fashion or lingerie items, wine, flowers, homeware and children's goods.

The delivery charge is variable. There are good features such as the running total, but the process of shopping is very slow.

www.boots.co.uk

ORIGIN	UK
SPEED	✓✓✓
INFO	✓✓✓✓
VALUE	✓✓✓
EASE	✓✓✓✓

A functional approach from Boots aimed at women but with a section for men. The site is split into two sections: information covers health and beauty plus product news; while the shop provides an excellent product range under sections covering health and beauty, and mother and baby. Delivery is free for orders over £60, below that there is a £2.95 charge. You can also use your Advantage card on some items.

www.whsmith.co.uk

ORIGIN	UK
SPEED	✓✓✓✓
INFO	✓✓✓✓✓
VALUE	✓✓✓
EASE	✓✓✓✓

Smiths are a family oriented internet service provider, which is reflected in the site, offering free web space, e-mail and cyber patrol (see page 144). On the whole it undersells its virtues, there is a great deal here, including:
1. Shopping, with offers on books in particular, but also on CDs, videos and games. Delivery charges differ between product types.
2. The Hutchinson Encyclopaedia, full access for Smiths' ISP users.
3. News, covering entertainment, sports and the book world.
4. An excellent education resource for children of all ages.

5. Information on computer technology and the internet.
6. Hints and tips on lifestyle with good links to health, gardening and other similar sites.

www.woolworths.co.uk

ORIGIN	UK
SPEED	✓✓
INFO	✓✓
VALUE	✓✓✓✓
EASE	✓✓✓✓

Not much of an offer from Woolworths, but there are some good bargains on toys and a Disney section. There's only a limited number of entertainment products to buy with free delivery on orders over £50. There is promise of a better selection of products to come but they will have to considerably upgrade the site if they are to be competitive.

www.argos.co.uk

ORIGIN	UK
SPEED	✓✓✓✓
INFO	✓✓✓✓
VALUE	✓✓✓✓
EASE	✓✓✓✓

Argos offer an excellent range of products across fourteen different categories as per their catalogue. There are some good bargains to be had but you have to search them out. Delivery is £3.95 unless you spend more than £150 in which case it's free.

The internet's general retailers and on-line departments

www.shopsmart.com
ON-LINE SHOPPING MADE SIMPLE

ORIGIN	UK
SPEED	✓✓✓✓
INFO	✓✓✓✓✓
VALUE	✓✓✓✓
EASE	✓✓✓✓✓

This is by far the best of the sites that offer links to specialist on-line retailers. Search within the sixteen categories or the whole site for a particular item or store. Each of the 1000 or so retail sites featured are reviewed and rated using a star system, the reviews are quite kind, and the worst sites are excluded anyway. Use their PriceScan system to locate the best prices. See also **www.shopandsave.com** who specialise in monitoring stores and highlighting those giving the best discounts.

www.mytaxi.co.uk

SHOP AND SEARCH FOR THE BEST PRICES

ORIGIN UK
SPEED ✓✓✓
INFO ✓✓✓✓
VALUE ✓✓✓✓
EASE ✓✓✓

Personalise your on-line shopping experience using My Taxi to search retailer's web sites for the best prices. Particularly strong on music and video, less so on other items. The recommended on-line stores are selected according to safety and service but there is no star rating system.

www.zoom.co.uk

MORE THAN JUST A SHOP

ORIGIN UK
SPEED ✓✓✓✓✓
INFO ✓✓✓
VALUE ✓✓✓
EASE ✓✓✓✓

This is an excellent magazine-style site, with lots of features other than shopping, such as free internet access, e-mail and a dating service. Shopping consists of links to specialist retailers. You can earn loyalty points, enter prize draws and there are a number of exclusive offers as well. Not always the cheapest, but an entertaining shopping site.

www.virgin.net

LIFESTYLE AND SHOPPING GUIDE

ORIGIN UK
SPEED ✓✓✓
INFO ✓✓✓✓✓
EASE ✓✓✓✓

Virgin's shopping guide is comprehensive, covering all major categories while allowing retailers to feature some of their best offers. It also attempts to be a complete service for entertainment and leisure needs with sections on music, travel and cinema.

www.shoppingunlimited.co.uk

INDEPENDENT RECOMMENDATION

ORIGIN UK
SPEED ✓✓✓✓
INFO ✓✓✓✓
VALUE ✓✓✓✓
EASE ✓✓✓✓✓

Owned by the *Guardian* newspaper, this site offers hundreds of links to stores that they've reviewed. It also offers help to inexperienced shoppers and guidance on using credit cards on-line. There are also links to other *Guardian* sites such as news and sport.

www.shoppersuniverse.co.uk
GREAT UNIVERSAL STORES

ORIGIN UK
SPEED ✓✓✓✓
INFO ✓✓✓✓
VALUE ✓✓✓✓
EASE ✓✓✓✓✓

Avoid having to shop around by using this clear and simple site that offers a wide variety of products at excellent value. It also hosts other stores too.

www.barclaysquare.co.uk
NOT JUST FOR BARCLAYCARD OWNERS

ORIGIN UK
SPEED ✓✓✓✓
INFO ✓✓✓
VALUE ✓✓✓✓
EASE ✓✓✓✓

Barclays site provides a set of links to preferred retailers, and is one of the oldest and most techno-logically advanced of on-line retailers. The selection of shops you can visit is quite limited compared to other similar sites, however, there are some good bargains, and you can be sure that there will be few problems with payment security. W?WT

www.bigsave.com
SAVE, SAVE, SAVE...

ORIGIN UK
SPEED ✓✓✓
INFO ✓✓✓
VALUE ✓✓✓✓✓
EASE ✓✓✓✓

Bigsave has six sections with an emphasis on value and, although there are over 7000 products to choose from, the choice feels limited. Registration is required, but you can track your purchase from order to delivery. Delivery costs vary according to product.

www.buckinghamgate.co.uk
THE BEST OF BRITISH QUALITY AND DESIGN

ORIGIN UK
SPEED ✓✓✓✓
INFO ✓✓✓✓
VALUE ✓✓
EASE ✓✓✓✓✓

Basically a selection of links to posh shops, or that's what it's supposed to look like, as a few are not quite that up-market. However, you can buy Rolls Royce merchandise, book a flight on British Airways or treat yourself to a weekend at a health farm. What ho! W?WT

www.buy-appointment.co.uk

FROM THE 7TH EARL OF BRADFORD

ORIGIN UK
SPEED ✓✓✓
INFO ✓✓✓✓
VALUE ✓✓✓
EASE ✓✓✓✓✓

Richard the 7th Earl of Bradford has organised this quality site in an attempt to put the excitement back into shopping. There is an excellent selection of quality products in over 30 shopping areas. Whilst the products have been chosen for their quality and value isn't a priority, delivery is free. **W?WT**

www.bsilly.com

NOTHING SILLY ABOUT FINDING THE BEST PRICES

ORIGIN US
SPEED ✓✓✓
INFO ✓✓✓
VALUE ✓✓✓✓
EASE ✓✓✓✓

Basically this is a shopping search engine. Go into one of the sixteen product sections and type in the description of an item, you then get the best price and the link to the relevant retailer. As it's American some products are not available in the UK.

http://orders.mkn.co.uk

THE NET MARKET

ORIGIN UK
SPEED ✓✓✓✓
INFO ✓✓
VALUE ✓✓✓
EASE ✓✓✓✓

A large collection of links to on-line stores and services that tend not to be listed in the major sites. Worth a look for something a little different.

www.letsbuyit.com

SAVE BY CO-BUYING

ORIGIN UK
SPEED ✓✓✓✓
INFO ✓✓✓✓
VALUE ✓✓✓
EASE ✓✓✓✓

The idea is that by buying co-operatively you can drive the price down of the products you request. It's great if you can rally friends and family who all want to buy the same thing – which is also its disadvantage – you all have the same thing. Prices often aren't that keen either. Still, as it expands it will improve with the buying power it gets.

www.ybag.com
LET SOMEONE ELSE DO THE SHOPPING

ORIGIN UK	Tell the Ybag team what you want and what you
SPEED ✓✓✓✓	want to pay, and then they put a seller in touch with
INFO ✓✓✓	you. As long as you don't put in requests at silly
VALUE ✓✓✓✓	prices you won't be disappointed, but be prepared
EASE ✓✓✓✓	for a wait.

Software

If you need to upgrade your software then these are the sites to go to.

www.softwareparadise.co.uk
THE SMART WAY TO SHOP FOR SOFTWARE

ORIGIN UK	With over 250,000 titles and excellent offers make
SPEED ✓✓✓✓	this site your first stop. It's easy-to-use, there's a
INFO ✓✓✓✓	good search facility and plenty of products for Mac
VALUE ✓✓✓	users. There are links to sister sites offering low cost
EASE ✓✓✓	software for charities and students. W?WT

See also: www.software-warehouse.co.uk W?WT
www.beyond.com.

www.bugnet.com
FIX THAT BUG

ORIGIN UK	Subscribe to the Bug net and they alert you to soft-
SPEED ✓✓✓	ware bugs, keep you up to date with reviews, analy-
INFO ✓✓✓	sis and the tests they carry out. You can then be sure
VALUE ✓✓✓✓	to buy the right fixes.
EASE ✓✓✓✓	

www.winzip.com
MANAGE FILES

ORIGIN US
SPEED ✓✓✓
INFO ✓✓✓✓
EASE ✓✓✓

Winzip allows you to save space on your PCs by compressing data, making it easier to e-mail files and unlock zipped files that have been sent to you. It takes a few minutes to download. For Macs go to www.aladdinsys.com.

Soap Operas

The official and unofficial sites for our major soap operas.

www.corrie.net
CORONATION STREET BY ITS FANS

ORIGIN UK
SPEED ✓✓✓✓
INFO ✓✓✓✓✓
EASE ✓✓✓✓✓

Corrie was formed in 1999 from several fans' sites and has no connection with Granada. The site is written by volunteer fans, who contribute articles, updates and biographies. There are five key sections:
1. One for Corrie newbies (are there any?) with a history of the Street.
2. A catch up with the story section.
3. What's up and coming.
4. Profiles on the key characters.
5. A chat section for Street gossip.
For a wackier view of the Street see www.csvu.net.

www.coronationstreet.co.uk
THE OFFICIAL CORONATION STREET

ORIGIN UK
SPEED ✓✓✓
INFO ✓✓✓✓
VALUE ✓✓
EASE ✓✓✓✓

This is the official site, and its split into six sections:
1. In the Underworld you can delve into the history of the Street with the ghost of Ena Sharples.
2. In the Kabin you can get sneak previews and get up to speed if you've missed an episode.

3. There are competitions at the Battersbys.
4. You can buy Corrie gifts at the Corner Shop.
5. Lastly you can get a history and virtual tour at Ken Barlow's.

The site is spoiled by the amount of advertising.

www.emmerdale.co.uk
THE OFFICIAL EMMERDALE SITE

ORIGIN UK
SPEED ✓✓
INFO ✓✓✓✓
VALUE ✓✓
EASE ✓✓✓✓

Very similar to the official *Coronation Street* site, you can:

1. Find out what's new in *Emmerdale* at the Village Hall.
2. Get village history and photos of your favourite characters at Keepers Cottage.
3. Visit The Woolpack for the latest gossip and competitions.
4. Check out the shop for *Emmerdale* merchandise or send a postcard.

The site is slow due to the constant advertising.

Both *Emmerdale* and *Coronation Street* are hosted by www.G-Wizz.com, who also host sites for Granada, Yorkshire TV, LWT and Tyne Tees television.

www.emmerdale.clara.net/emmerdale.html
THE UNOFFICIAL EMMERDALE SITE

ORIGIN UK
SPEED ✓✓✓
INFO ✓✓✓
EASE ✓✓✓✓

An eccentric site run by a consummate fan with a less fussy approach than the official site. It is divided up into sections in which you can see things such as "spot the out-take". There are links to other *Emmerdale* fan sites, a weekly poll, a message board and you can send a postcard.

www.bbc.co.uk/eastenders
THE OFFICIAL EASTENDERS PAGE

ORIGIN UK
SPEED ✓✓✓✓
INFO ✓✓✓✓
EASE ✓✓✓✓

A page from the massive BBC site split into several sections:
1. Catch up on the latest stories.
2. Get hints on future storylines.
3. Play games and competitions.
4. Get pictures of the stars.
5. Vote in their latest poll.
6. Reminisce in the "Remember When" section.
7. Take a virtual tour and view Albert Square with the Walford Cam.

www.brookie.com
THE OFFICIAL BROOKSIDE WEB SITE

ORIGIN UK
SPEED ✓✓
INFO ✓✓✓✓
EASE ✓✓✓

You have two options, either the highly animated version or the one with fewer pictures and no sound. Either will give you all the latest information, gossip or storyline with plenty of background on the cast. There are competitions and you can shop for Brookie merchandise. With the animated version you can download clips and take a virtual tour, but be patient. Also the sound effects are really annoying.

www.hollyoaks.com
THE OFFICIAL HOLLYOAKS WEB SITE

ORIGIN UK
SPEED ✓✓
INFO ✓✓
EASE ✓✓✓✓

A much more basic, and less enjoyable site than *Brookside*, it offers information on Phil Redmond who created both programs, the story so far, character info and a feedback section.

www.baxendale.u-net.com/ramsayst/
NEIGHBOURS WORLDWIDE FANPAGES

ORIGIN UK
SPEED ✓✓
INFO ✓✓✓✓
EASE ✓✓✓

You can also get them at **www.ramsay-street.co.uk**. This is a labour of love by the fans of *Neighbours*, and has everything you need:
1. Storylines past, present and future.
2. Information on all the characters.
3. Clips from some episodes.
4. Complete discographies of the singing stars.
5. Access to all the related web sites through the links page.

Unfortunately you can't buy merchandise from the site.

www.seven.com.au/homeandaway/
THE OFFICIAL HOME AND AWAY SITE

ORIGIN AUSTRALIA
SPEED ✓✓✓
INFO ✓✓✓✓
EASE ✓✓✓

As you'd expect, a bright and breezy site, in which you can learn all the facts about the characters that inhabit Summer Bay. You can:
1. Download pictures of the cast.
2. Learn the lyrics of the theme tune.
3. Visit the past episode archives.
4. E-mail the cast.

www.alkenmrs.com
LICENSED TELEVISION MEMORABILIA

ORIGIN UK
SPEED ✓✓
INFO ✓✓✓
VALUE ✓✓
EASE ✓✓✓✓

Alken has a selection of products, books and videos covering *Coronation Street, Emmerdale, Home and Away, Eastenders* and also *Heartbeat* and *Ballykissangel*. Shipping is £3 for the UK.

Sport

One of the best uses of the internet is to keep up to date with how your team is performing, or if you're a member of a team or association, keep each other updated.

General sports sites

www.sporting-life.com
THE SPORTING LIFE

ORIGIN UK
SPEED ✓✓✓✓
INFO ✓✓✓✓
EASE ✓✓✓✓

A very comprehensive sport site, with plenty of advice, tips, news and latest scores, it's considered to be one of the best. It's very good for stories, in-depth analysis, and overall coverage of the major sports.

www.sports.com
SPORTS NEWS AND SHOPPING

ORIGIN UK
SPEED ✓✓✓
INFO ✓✓✓✓
VALUE ✓✓✓
EASE ✓✓✓✓✓

More international in feel than Sporting Life, sports.com offers much in the way of information on all key sports, particularly football, in tandem with a shopping service mainly covering cricket, football and golf.

www.sky.com/sports/home
THE BEST OF SKY SPORT

ORIGIN UK
SPEED ✓✓✓✓
INFO ✓✓✓✓
EASE ✓✓✓✓

Excellent for the Premiership and football in general, but also covers other sports very well particularly cricket and both forms of Rugby. Includes a section featuring video and audio clips, and interviews with stars. You can vote in their polls or try sports trivia quizzes.

www.talksport.net

HOME OF TALK SPORT RADIO

ORIGIN	UK
SPEED	✓✓✓
INFO	✓✓✓✓
VALUE	✓✓
EASE	✓✓✓✓

Listen to sports news and debate while you work, the information comes from Sporting Life but it's up to date. There's also an audio archive and scheduling information.

The BBC offer superb sports coverage from their own web site **www.bbc.co.uk/sport**.

Archery

www.archery.org

INTERNATIONAL ARCHERY FEDERATION

ORIGIN	UK
SPEED	✓✓
INFO	✓✓✓
EASE	✓✓✓✓

Get the news, events listings and records information from this fairly mundane site and learn more about field archery at **www.fieldarcher.com**, which has a great enthusiastic amateur feel.

Athletics

www.athletix.gr

WORLD ATHLETICS NEWS

ORIGIN	GREECE
SPEED	✓✓✓✓
INFO	✓✓✓✓✓
EASE	✓✓✓✓

This is an excellent, comprehensive site that is easy-to-use and covers all aspects of the sport. There are reports on each Grand Prix and event, with statistics and links to other sites. To see what Linford Christie is up to go to **www.nuff-respect.co.uk**.

www.runnersworld.com

RUNNER'S WORLD MAGAZINE

ORIGIN	US
SPEED	✓✓✓
INFO	✓✓✓✓
EASE	✓✓✓✓

A rather dry site with tips from getting started through to advanced running. There's lots of information, news and records, reviews on shoes and gear.

Basketball

www.nba.com

NATIONAL BASKETBALL ASSOCIATION

ORIGIN US
SPEED ✓✓✓
INFO ✓✓✓✓✓
EASE ✓✓✓✓

A very informative and comprehensive official site, with features on the teams, players and games; there's also an excellent photo gallery and you can watch some of the most important points if you have the right software. For the official line on British basketball go to www.bbl.org.uk, or www.britball.com which is unofficial but more fun.

Boxing

www.boxingonline.com

AT THE RINGSIDE

ORIGIN US
SPEED ✓✓
INFO ✓✓✓✓
EASE ✓✓✓✓

A combination of information and the latest technology make Boxing on-line a great website. There's loads of interviews, news and feature stories as well as events listings. You can also download fight extracts in both audio and video formats.

For the different boxing authorities:

WBA – www.wbaonline.com
WBC – www.ajapa.qc.ca/wbc/index/html
WBF – www.worldboxingfed.com
WBU – www.btinternet.com/wbuboxing
For women's boxing got to www.femboxer.com.

www.houseofboxing.com

HOME FOR BOXING ON THE NET

ORIGIN US
SPEED ✓✓✓
INFO ✓✓✓✓
EASE ✓✓✓✓

A beautifully designed site that gives comprehensive coverage on the world of boxing, including video interviews, reviews and features.

Bowls

www.lawnbowls.co.uk
PROMOTING THE GAME OF BOWLS

ORIGIN UK
SPEED ✓✓✓✓
INFO ✓✓✓✓
EASE ✓✓✓

Not just for lawn bowling, this site attempts to cover all types of bowls. It's being worked on, but its poor design makes it annoying to use, however there is plenty of news and a good set of links to other sites.

www.bowlsengland.com
ENGLISH BOWLING ASSOCIATION

ORIGIN UK
SPEED ✓✓
INFO ✓✓✓✓
EASE ✓✓✓

Again, poor design lets the site down, but if you persevere you'll find all you need to know about lawn bowls in England.

www.bowlsclubs.co.uk
INFORMATION ON BOWLING CLUBS

ORIGIN UK
SPEED ✓✓
INFO ✓✓✓✓
EASE ✓✓

Looks like poor web site design is common to all bowls sites, this one gives information on clubs and bowls news. It's strength is a good set of links to other bowls sites.

Cricket

www.uk.cricket.org or www.cricinfo.com
THE HOME OF CRICKET ON THE NET

ORIGIN UK
SPEED ✓✓✓✓
INFO ✓✓✓✓✓
VALUE ✓✓✓
EASE ✓✓✓✓

Simply the best cricket site on the internet bar none. In-depth analysis, match reports, player profiles, statistics, links to other more specialised sites and live written commentary. There's also a shop with lots of cricket goodies and delivery is included in the price.

www.khel.com

WORLD CRICKET

ORIGIN INDIA   Another site for the real fan, it's particularly good
SPEED ✓✓✓✓   for looking up statistics whether it is on players or
INFO ✓✓✓✓✓   matches, and it has a comprehensive set of links to
EASE ✓✓✓✓   other cricket sites. A real labour of love.

www.wisden.com

WISDEN CRICKET MONTHLY

ORIGIN UK   The best features from the magazine, created in
SPEED ✓✓✓✓   association with the *Guardian* and its excellent
INFO ✓✓✓✓   cricket site www.cricketunlimited.co.uk, some of the
EASE ✓✓✓✓   best cricket journalism you can get.

www.lords.org

THE OFFICIAL LINE ON CRICKET

ORIGIN UK   There's news, links to governing bodies, associations
SPEED ✓✓✓   and the MCC and ECB, combined with plenty of
INFO ✓✓✓✓✓   information about the game and players, even a
EASE ✓✓✓✓   quiz. It also has an excellent section on women's
   cricket. If you have RealPlayer, there's access to live
   games on audio via the BBC.

www.webbsoc.demon.co.uk

WOMEN'S CRICKET ON THE WEB

ORIGIN UK   There are not many sites about women's cricket, this
SPEED ✓✓✓✓   is probably the best, with features, news, fixture
INFO ✓✓✓✓   lists, match reports and player profiles. Nothing
EASE ✓✓✓   fancy, but it works.

Cycling

www.bcf.uk.com/
BRITISH CYCLING FEDERATION

ORIGIN UK
SPEED ✓
INFO ✓✓✓
EASE ✓✓✓

The governing body for cycling, the site is under development but you can still get information on events, rules, clubs and rankings.

www.bikemagic.com
IT'S BIKETASTIC!

ORIGIN UK
SPEED ✓✓✓
INFO ✓✓✓✓
VALUE ✓✓✓
EASE ✓✓✓✓

Whether you're a beginner or an old hand, the enthusiastic and engaging tone of this site will convert you or enhance your cycling experience. There's plenty of news and features, as well as reviews on bike parts and gadgets. There's also a classified ads section and a selection of links to other biking web sites all of which are rated.

Darts

www.embassydarts.com
EMBASSY WORLD DARTS

ORIGIN UK
SPEED ✓✓✓✓
INFO ✓✓✓✓✓
EASE ✓✓✓✓

Whether you think darts qualifies as a sport or not, this well designed site gives a great deal of information about the game, its players and the tournament. See also **www.cyberdarts.com** for more information and good links to other darts sites. For some outstanding advice on how to play the game visit the labour of love that is **www.dartbase.com**.

Equestrian

www.equestrianonline.com
EQUESTRIANS ON-LINE

ORIGIN UK
SPEED ✓✓✓
INFO ✓✓✓✓✓
EASE ✓✓✓

Get all the news and results on the sport with a bookstore, articles by those involved, profiles of the riders, owners and trainers, training tips and forums on each event.

Fishing

www.fishing.org
HOME OF UK FISHING ON THE NET

ORIGIN UK
SPEED ✓✓
INFO ✓✓✓✓✓
VALUE ✓✓
EASE ✓✓✓✓

A huge site that offers information on where to fish, how to fish, where's the best place to stay near fish, even fishing holidays. There's also advice on equipment, a records section and links to shops and shop locations. Shop on-site for fishing books and magazines. See also www.anglersnet.co.uk for good writing and for more information www.services-online.co.uk/angling.

Football

www.footballnews.co.uk
MORE COVERAGE THAN THE MILLENNIUM DOME

ORIGIN UK
SPEED ✓✓
INFO ✓✓✓✓✓
VALUE ✓✓
EASE ✓✓✓✓

For depth of coverage this is hard to beat – and they've got Des Lynam. It's less cluttered and easier to use than most other football sites, it's also up-to-date and doesn't miss much.

See also www.football365.co.uk and www.soccer-age.com which is excellent for world football, and the famous www.soccernet.com. For sheer flashiness, but with good competitions and kids sections go to

www.zoofootball.com For very good writing and
sports journalism try www.footballunlimited.co.uk.

www.ukfootballpages.com
IT'S WHERE YOU FIND FOOTBALL

ORIGIN UK
SPEED ✓✓✓✓
INFO ✓✓✓✓✓
EASE ✓✓✓✓

This site offers a huge directory of football related
links and boasts some 1200 enquiries a day; also
offers match reports and statistics.

www.teamtalk.com
CHECK OUT THE TEAMS!

ORIGIN UK
SPEED ✓✓✓
INFO ✓✓✓✓
EASE ✓✓✓✓

The place to go if you want all the latest gossip and
transfer information, it's opinionated but not often
wrong.

www.soccerbase.com
SOCCER STATISTICS

ORIGIN UK
SPEED ✓✓✓
INFO ✓✓✓✓✓
EASE ✓✓✓✓

The site to end all pub rows, it's described as the
most comprehensive and up-to-date source of British
football data on the internet.

Golf

www.golftoday.co.uk
THE PREMIER ON-LINE GOLF MAGAZINE

ORIGIN UK
SPEED ✓✓✓
INFO ✓✓✓✓✓
EASE ✓✓✓✓

An excellent site for golf news and tournaments
with features, statistics and rankings and also a
course directory. It's the best all-round site covering
Europe. There are also links to sister sites about the
amateur game, shops and where to stay.

www.golfweb.com
PGA TOUR

ORIGIN UK	The best site for statistics on the game, and keeping
SPEED ✓✓✓	up with tournament scores, it also has audio and
INFO ✓✓✓✓✓	visual features with RealPlayer. For the official word
EASE ✓✓✓✓	on the tour go to www.pga.com.

www.golf.com
THE AMERICAN VIEW

ORIGIN US	Part of NBC's suite of web sites, this offers a
SPEED ✓✓✓	massive amount of information on the game and
INFO ✓✓✓✓✓	players, both men and women.
EASE ✓✓✓	

Hockey

www.fieldhockey.com
HOCKEY NEWS

ORIGIN UK	All the information, news and games round-ups,
SPEED ✓✓✓✓	there's also good archive material, up-to-date rules
INFO ✓✓✓✓	and sections for coaches. For links go to
EASE ✓✓✓	http://hockey.enschede.com/uk/links.htm.

Horse Racing

www.racingpost.co.uk
THE RACING POST

ORIGIN UK	Superbly informative site from the authority on the
SPEED ✓✓	sport, every event covered in-depth with tips and
INFO ✓✓✓✓✓	advice. To get the best out of it you have to register,
EASE ✓✓✓✓	then you gain access to the database and more. For
	more information on the sport go to the British Horse
	Racing Board's excellent site at www.bhb.co.uk.

Ice Hockey

www.iceweb.co.uk
THE SEKONDA ICE HOCKEY LEAGUE

ORIGIN UK	Keep up-to-date with the scores, the games and the
SPEED ✓✓✓✓	players, even their injuries. Good for statistics as
INFO ✓✓✓✓✓	well as news. For more news see **www.azhockey.com**.
EASE ✓✓✓	

www.nhl.com
NATIONAL HOCKEY LEAGUE

ORIGIN US	Catch up on the latest from the NHL including a
SPEED ✓✓✓✓	chance to listen and watch key moments from past
INFO ✓✓✓✓	and recent games.
EASE ✓✓✓	

Marshal arts

www.martial-arts-network.com
PROMOTING MARTIAL ARTS

ORIGIN US	Possibly qualifies as the loudest introduction
SPEED ✓✓	sequence, but once you've cut the volume, the site
INFO ✓✓✓✓	offers a great deal in terms of resources and infor-
EASE ✓✓✓	mation about the martial arts scene. Sadly it's over
	engineered, making it slow and a little confusing to use.

Motor sport

www.ukmotorsport.com
INFORMATION OVERLOAD

ORIGIN UK	This site, a great advert for function over design,
SPEED ✓✓✓✓	covers every form of motor racing. It's easy-to-use
INFO ✓✓✓✓✓	and thorough, with lots of links to appropriate sites.
EASE ✓✓✓✓	

www.linksheaven.com

THE MOST COMPREHENSIVE LINKS DIRECTORY

ORIGIN US
SPEED ✓✓✓
INFO ✓✓✓✓✓
EASE ✓✓✓✓

Whatever, whoever, there's an appropriate link. It concentrates on Formula 1, CART and Nascar though.

www.autosport.com

AUTOSPORT MAGAZINE

ORIGIN UK
SPEED ✓✓
INFO ✓✓✓✓✓
VALUE ✓✓✓
EASE ✓✓✓

Excellent for news and features on motor sport plus links and a slightly confusing on-line shopping experience for related products such as team gear, books or models.

www.rallysport.com

COVERING THE WORLD RALLY CHAMPIONSHIP

ORIGIN UK
SPEED ✓✓✓✓
INFO ✓✓✓
VALUE ✓✓✓
EASE ✓✓✓✓

Good for results and news on rallying across the world and in the UK. See also www.rallyzone.co.uk which is a rapidly developing alternative.

www.btcc.co.uk

BRITISH TOURING CAR CHAMPIONSHIP

ORIGIN UK
SPEED ✓✓✓
INFO ✓✓✓✓✓
EASE ✓✓✓✓

An exciting site that offers a great deal of information and statistics on the championship, driver and team profiles, photos and links to other related sites.

www.fosa.org

FORMULA ONE SUPPORTERS ASSOCIATION

ORIGIN UK
SPEED ✓✓
INFO ✓✓✓
VALUE ✓✓
EASE ✓✓✓✓

An F1 enthusiast's site, set up by fans to provide feedback to the people who run the sport. It's informative and there's plenty of quizzes, statistics and articles, even a tour of a racing car from Prost.

www.itv-f1.com
F1 ON ITV

ORIGIN UK
SPEED ✓✓✓✓
INFO ✓✓✓✓✓
EASE ✓✓✓✓✓

The TV show may be disappointing, but the web site is excellent. There's all the background information you'd expect plus circuit profiles, schedules and a photo gallery. For more news and links to everywhere in F1 go to **www.f1-world.co.uk**.

Mountaineering and outdoor sports

www.mountainzone.com
FOR THE UPWARDLY MOBILE

ORIGIN US
SPEED ✓✓✓
INFO ✓✓✓✓✓
EASE ✓✓✓

Thoroughly covers all aspects of climbing, hiking, mountain biking, skiing and snowboarding, with a very good photography section featuring galleries from major mountains and climbers. There's also a store offering gear at discount prices but shipping is expensive so try **www.rockandrun.co.uk**. W?WT

Olympics

www.olympics.org
BRITISH OLYMPIC ASSOCIATION

ORIGIN UK
SPEED ✓✓✓✓
INFO ✓✓✓
EASE ✓✓✓✓

Background on the work of the BOA and the team, also has information on the medallists, as well as history and education pages. You can even book a team member as an after-dinner speaker.

www.olympics.com
OFFICIAL SYDNEY GAMES SITE

ORIGIN AUS
SPEED ✓✓✓✓
INFO ✓✓✓✓
EASE ✓✓✓✓

All the information on the Sydney games, the key players, news, what's on and when, plus history, the countries taking part and a section on the Paralympics. See also **www.olympics2000.co.uk**.

Rowing

www.ara-rowing.org
AMATEUR ROWING ASSOCIATION

ORIGIN UK	This site offers information on the history of the
SPEED ✓✓	sport, plus the latest news, coaching tips and links.
INFO ✓✓✓	Some of it is still under development, for better
VALUE ✓✓	links go to http://users.ox.ac.uk/~quarell.
EASE ✓✓✓✓	

Rugby

www.scrum.com
THE RUGBY WEB SITE

ORIGIN UK	An excellent, comprehensive site about rugby union
SPEED ✓✓	with impressively up-to-the-minute coverage. For a
INFO ✓✓✓	similar but lighter site go to www.planet-rugby.com.
EASE ✓✓✓✓	

www.rugbyrugby.com
WORLD RUGBY

ORIGIN NZ	Amazingly comprehensive round-up of world rugby
SPEED ✓✓✓	with instant reports, lots of detail and information
INFO ✓✓✓✓✓	on both union and league. There's also a shop with
VALUE ✓✓	a small selection of gear, which is very expensive
EASE ✓✓✓✓	when you add delivery charges.

www.irb.org
INTERNATIONAL RUGBY BOARD

ORIGIN UK	For the official line on rugby union. There's the rules
SPEED ✓✓✓	and regulations explained, information on world
INFO ✓✓✓✓	tournaments, history of the game and some good
EASE ✓✓✓✓	articles from *Oval World* magazine.

www.rleague.com
WORLD OF RUGBY LEAGUE

ORIGIN UK
SPEED ✓✓✓
INFO ✓✓✓✓✓
EASE ✓✓✓✓

Another very comprehensive site, featuring sections on Australia, New Zealand and the UK, with plenty of chat, articles, player profiles and enough statistics to keep the most ardent fan happy.

Skiing and Snowboarding

www.fis-ski.com
INTERNATIONAL SKI FEDERATION

ORIGIN US
SPEED ✓✓✓
INFO ✓✓✓✓
EASE ✓✓✓✓

Catch up on the news, the fastest times, and the rankings in all forms of skiing at this site. Very good background information and an excellent picture gallery sets the whole thing off. For the more rugged, there is also the very well written http://mountainzone.com.

www.ski.co.uk
THE PLACE TO START – A SKI DIRECTORY

ORIGIN UK
SPEED ✓✓✓
INFO ✓✓✓✓
EASE ✓✓✓✓

Not exactly state-of-the-art web design, but the information in the directory is useful and the recommended sites are rated. The sections are holidays, travel, weather, resorts, snowboarding, gear, fanatics and specialist services.

www.natives.co.uk
NATIVES OF THE MOUNTAINS

ORIGIN UK
SPEED ✓✓✓✓
INFO ✓✓✓✓
VALUE ✓✓
EASE ✓✓✓✓

The hippest of ski sites with information on conditions, ski resorts, jobs, where to stay and links to other cool sites all wrapped up in a very nicely designed site.

www.1ski.com
COMPLETE ON-LINE SKIING SERVICE

ORIGIN UK
SPEED ✓✓✓
INFO ✓✓✓✓✓
VALUE ✓✓✓
EASE ✓✓✓✓

With over 43,000 holidays, live snow reports, tips on technique and equipment and the ultimate guide featuring over 750 resorts it's difficult to go wrong. There's a good events calendar too. See also the similar **www.iglu.com** who offer 3D mapping as part of their service.

Considered one of the most comprehensive of the skiing sites, **www.complete-skier.com** has a very good holiday booking service.
www.skimaps.com is much like any other general ski site except for its eponymous maps section.

www.snowboardinguk.co.uk
UK SNOWBOARDING NEWS

ORIGIN UK
SPEED ✓✓✓
INFO ✓✓✓✓✓
EASE ✓✓✓✓

A surprisingly unpretentious site for what is the coolest of sports, aimed at anyone whether beginner or expert, it offers news, an events diary, resort information, travel information and a links page. For the expected naffness go to "Feel the powder" **www.feelthepow.com**, which is only good for its tips section. For the best board shopping try **www.legendsboardriders.com**.

Snooker

www.snookernet.com
ALL ABOUT SNOOKER

ORIGIN UK
SPEED ✓✓✓
INFO ✓✓✓✓
VALUE ✓✓✓
EASE ✓✓✓✓✓

A clearly laid out, easy-to-use site that has comprehensive information on the game, plus a master class from a top player, links, a shop selling snooker merchandise, a club finder and subscription to *SnookerScene* magazine. From the sponsor, visit www.embassysnooker.com who have a similar but less comprehensive site.

Tennis and racquet sports

www.lta.org.uk
LAWN TENNIS ASSOCIATION

ORIGIN UK	An excellent all-year tennis information site run by
SPEED ✓✓✓	the Lawn Tennis Association. It has information on
INFO ✓✓✓✓	the players, rankings and tournament news, as well
EASE ✓✓✓✓	as details on clubs and coaching courses. See also
	www.atptour.com, which is less UK-biased.

www.tennis.org.uk
THE TENNIS SEARCH ENGINE

ORIGIN UK	You can search a mass of good tennis links, plus get
SPEED ✓✓✓✓	all the results information and stats. Straight
INFO ✓✓✓✓	forward and easy-to-use.
EASE ✓✓✓✓	

www.wimbledon.org
THE OFFICIAL WIMBLEDON SITE

ORIGIN UK	Very impressive, there's a great deal here and not just
SPEED ✓✓	in June, but you need to be patient. Apart from the
INFO ✓✓✓✓	information you'd expect, you can download screen-
VALUE ✓✓	savers, visit the on-line museum and eventually see
EASE ✓✓✓✓	videos of past matches. The shop is expensive.

www.badmintonuk.ndo.co.uk
BRITISH BADMINTON

ORIGIN UK	A clear, easy-to-use site packed with information
SPEED ✓✓✓✓	about badminton, how ladders work, directory of
INFO ✓✓✓✓	coaches, club directory, rules, but not much news on
EASE ✓✓✓✓	the game. For that go to www.baofe.co.uk, the site
	of the Badminton Association of England. For sheer
	attitude try www.realbadminton.co.uk.

www.squashplayer.co.uk

WORLD OF SQUASH AT YOUR FINGERTIPS

ORIGIN US
SPEED ✓✓✓✓
VALUE ✓✓✓✓✓
EASE ✓✓✓✓✓

A really comprehensive round-up of the game, with links galore and a great news section, there's also a section for the UK, which has club details and the latest news.

www.ettu.org

EUROPEAN TABLE TENNIS UNION

ORIGIN UK
SPEED ✓✓✓
INFO ✓✓✓✓
EASE ✓✓✓✓

Find out about the ETTU, its rankings, competition details and results plus a section devoted to world table tennis links. See also **www.ittf.com**, which gives a world view.

Water sports and swimming

www.swimnet.co.uk

ALL YOU NEED TO KNOW ABOUT SWIMMING

ORIGIN UK
SPEED ✓✓✓✓
INFO ✓✓✓✓✓
EASE ✓✓✓✓

The best site for information on swimming in the UK, this offers details on the major events, news, profiles and videos of the best swimmers and races.

www.stormrider.co.uk

ULTIMATE GUIDE FOR SURFING THE UK COAST

ORIGIN UK
SPEED ✓✓✓
INFO ✓✓✓
EASE ✓✓✓✓

Includes forecasts for weather and surf, satellite images, live surf web cams from around the world and a complete directory of surfing web sites. For a more traditional and regional approach try **www.surfcall.co.uk**.

www.waterski.com
WORLD OF WATER SKIING

ORIGIN US	An American site which features information about
SPEED ✓✓✓	the sport, how to compete, news, tips, equipment
INFO ✓✓✓✓	and where to ski. See also www.waterski-az.co.uk.
EASE ✓✓✓✓	

Sports clothes and merchandise

www.kitbag.com
SPORTS FASHION

ORIGIN UK	Football kits and gear galore from new to retro;
SPEED ✓✓✓	covers cricket and rugby too. Free delivery.
INFO ✓✓✓✓	
VALUE ✓✓✓	
EASE ✓✓✓✓	

www.discountsports.co.uk
UK'S LOWEST PRICED SPORTSWEAR

ORIGIN UK	Cheap and cheerful approach, with all the major
SPEED ✓✓✓	brands represented and much of what they offer has
INFO ✓✓✓	free delivery in the UK. **W?WT**
VALUE ✓✓✓✓	
EASE ✓✓✓✓	

www.fatface.co.uk
FASHION LEISURE AND SPORTS WEAR

ORIGIN UK	Good range and returns policy from this fashionable
SPEED ✓✓	looking site with specific sections for kids and girls.
INFO ✓✓✓✓	As with most designer gear, it can be a little expensive.
VALUE ✓✓✓	
EASE ✓✓✓✓	

www.sportspages.co.uk
TAKING SPORT SERIOUSLY

ORIGIN UK	Book and video specialists, concentrating on sport,
SPEED ✓✓✓✓	they offer a wide range at OK prices. Great for that
INFO ✓✓✓✓	one thing you've been unable to find.
VALUE ✓✓	
EASE ✓✓✓✓	

Stamp Collecting

see Hobbies

Supermarkets

see Food and Drink

Telecommunications

www.carphonewarehouse.com

UNBIASED INFORMATION ABOUT MOBILES

ORIGIN	UK	Find the best tariff using their calculator, then take
SPEED	✓✓✓	advantage of the numerous offers. Excellent pictures
INFO	✓✓✓✓	and details of all phones. Delivery is free. Another
VALUE	✓✓✓	good site is **www.miahtelecom.co.uk** who, apart from
EASE	✓✓✓✓	good offers, have an easy-to-use tariff calculator.

www.anywhereyougo.com

WAP TECHNOLOGY EXPLAINED

ORIGIN	UK	Previously known as waptastic.com, it features
SPEED	✓✓✓	wireless application protocol, which will change the
INFO	✓✓✓✓	use and nature of mobile phones, enabling you to
EASE	✓✓✓✓	access the internet from virtually anywhere. It's in

its infancy and this is a good place to start. Also try
www.wapaw.com. To use WAP from your PC you
need a WAP emulator, one of the best of which is
found at **http://updev.phone.com**.

www.phonebills.org

HOW MUCH CAN YOU SAVE ON PHONE BILLS?

ORIGIN	UK	Find out the true cost of using the internet and the
SPEED	✓✓✓✓✓	phone, then find the best package to suit you. All
INFO	✓✓✓✓✓	you have to do is set it up.
EASE	✓✓✓✓✓	

Theatre

www.theatrenet.com
THE ENTERTAINMENT CENTRE

ORIGIN UK
SPEED ✓✓✓
INFO ✓✓✓✓✓
VALUE ✓✓✓
EASE ✓✓✓✓

Get the latest news, catch the new shows and, if you join the club, there are discounts on tickets for theatre, concerts, sporting events and holidays. You can also search their archives for information on past productions. See also the UK Theatre Web at www.uktw.co.uk who also offer information on amateur dramatics, jobs and just gossip.

www.rsc.org.uk
THE ROYAL SHAKESPEARE COMPANY

ORIGIN UK
SPEED ✓✓✓
INFO ✓✓✓✓
EASE ✓✓✓

Get all the news as well as information on performances and tours. You can book tickets on-line although it's via a third party site. There is also a shop in development.

To book on-line try the following sites:
www.ticketmaster.co.uk
www.londontheatretickets.com
www.uktickets.co.uk
www.lastminute.com
www.firstcall.co.uk.

Toys

see Children

Train Tickets

see Travel and Holidays – Britain

Transport

Aircraft

www.flyer.co.uk
AVIATION IN THE UK

ORIGIN UK
SPEED ✓✓✓
INFO ✓✓✓✓✓
EASE ✓✓✓✓

News, views and information about the world of aviation from the *Flyer Magazine* site, there's a good section on aviation links, and how to buy and sell an aircraft, classified ads and even free internet access.

www.aeroflight.co.uk
AVIATION ENTHUSIASTS

ORIGIN UK
SPEED ✓✓✓
INFO ✓✓✓✓✓
EASE ✓✓✓✓

An expanding site that attempts to offer an information stop for all aviation enthusiasts. It has details on the world's air forces, air shows and museums, and a section on the media with specialist books and bookshops.

www.airdisaster.com
NO.1 AVIATION SAFETY RESOURCE

ORIGIN UK
SPEED ✓✓✓
INFO ✓✓✓✓✓
EASE ✓✓✓✓

A rather macabre site that reviews each major air crash, and looks into the reasons behind what happened. It's not for the squeamish, but the cockpit voice recordings and eyewitness accounts make fascinating, if somewhat moving reading.

http://catalogue.janes.com/jawa.shtml
JANES DEFENCE INFORMATION

ORIGIN UK
SPEED ✓✓✓
INFO ✓✓✓✓✓
VALUE ✓✓✓
EASE ✓✓✓

Janes are the authority on military information, and you can download (with monthly updates) their All the World's Aircraft list for £840, or buy on CD-Rom for £765. For their homepage go to www.janesonline.com.

Bicycles

www.cycleweb.co.uk
THE INTERNET CYCLING CLUB

ORIGIN UK	An attempt to bring together all things cycling
SPEED ✓✓✓✓	aimed at a general audience rather than cycling as a
INFO ✓✓✓✓✓	sport. You have to pay a small fee to join the club,
VALUE ✓✓✓	but access to most of the information is free.
EASE ✓✓✓	

www.bicyclenet.co.uk
UK's NUMBER 1 ON-LINE BICYCLE SHOP

ORIGIN UK	Great selection of bikes and accessories to buy with
SPEED ✓✓✓	free delivery to anywhere in the UK. There's also
INFO ✓✓✓	good advice on how to buy the right bike and
VALUE ✓✓✓	they're flexible about method of payment.
EASE ✓✓✓	

www.cycling.uk.com
THE CYCLING INFORMATION STATION

ORIGIN UK	A fairly basic site with links to over 200 cycling web
SPEED ✓✓✓✓	sites collected under headings such as holidays,
INFO ✓✓✓✓	legal, tracks, museums, books and events.
EASE ✓✓✓✓	

Cars

www.dvla.gov.uk
DRIVER AND VEHICLE LICENSING AGENCY

ORIGIN UK	Excellent for the official line in motoring, the
SPEED ✓✓✓	driver's section has details on penalty points, licence
INFO ✓✓✓✓✓	changes and medical issues. The vehicles section
VALUE ✓✓✓	goes through all related forms and there's also a
EASE ✓✓✓	what's new page. It's well written throughout and
	information is easy to find. See also
	www.theaa.co.uk, www.rac.co.uk, and
	www.greenflag.co.uk.

www.autoexpress.co.uk
THE BEST MOTORING NEWS AND INFORMATION

ORIGIN UK
SPEED ✓✓
INFO ✓✓✓✓✓
EASE ✓✓✓✓

Massive database on cars, with motoring news and features on the latest models. You can check prices too. It also has classified ads and a great set of links. Register to get access to most of the information.

www.whatcar.co.uk
BRITAIN'S NUMBER 1 BUYER'S GUIDE

ORIGIN UK
SPEED ✓✓✓
INFO ✓✓✓✓✓
VALUE ✓✓✓
EASE ✓✓✓✓

A neatly packaged, one-stop shop for cars with sections on buying, selling, news, features and road tests. The classified section has thousands of cars and an easy-to-use search facility. See also **www.testcar.com**.

www.autotrader.com
YOUR CAR IS WAITING

ORIGIN UK
SPEED ✓✓✓
INFO ✓✓✓✓✓
VALUE ✓✓✓
EASE ✓✓✓✓

Claiming over 1.5 million listings for cars and parts, it's easy-to-use and there's good financial information. Other sites with virtual car sales are **www.autolocate.co.uk** and **www.carseller.co.uk**.

www.autobytel.co.uk
WORLD'S LEADING INTERNET-BASED NEW AND USED CAR BUYING SERVICE

ORIGIN US/UK
SPEED ✓✓✓✓
INFO ✓✓✓✓✓
VALUE ✓✓✓✓
EASE ✓✓✓

The easy way to buy a car on-line, just select the model you want then follow the on-line instructions. They will get quotes from local dealers and there are detailed descriptions and photos. There's also financial information.

www.carbusters.com
BUY WITH WHICH? MAGAZINE

ORIGIN UK   *Which?* make it easy to buy a new car from Europe
SPEED ✓✓✓✓   at a substantial discount. It's easy-to-use and there's
INFO ✓✓✓✓✓   lots of guidance and reassurance about the process.
VALUE ✓✓✓✓✓   You are better off joining as a *Which?* member as
EASE ✓✓✓✓   the fees are much cheaper. W?WT

www.totalise.net/eurekar/index.htm
SAVE MONEY BY IMPORTING FROM EUROPE

ORIGIN UK   Eurekar is a venture set up by the ISP Totalise to
SPEED ✓✓✓   import cheaper right-hand-drive cars from Europe.
INFO ✓✓✓✓✓   They claim to save up to 40% off UK prices. The
VALUE ✓✓✓✓   choice of cars is limited, but all are inspected by
EASE ✓✓✓   Green Flag and have a warranty. Totalise offer
quotes inclusive of VAT, delivery and duties.

For more car buying information and cars for
sale try:

www.fish4cars.co.uk – over 200,000 cars on their
database, plus hundreds of other vehicles.

www.carsource.co.uk – great for data and on-line
quotes.

www.carnet-online.co.uk/haynes/index.html
HAYNES MANUALS

ORIGIN UK   Download any Haynes car manual to help with
SPEED ✓✓✓✓   repairs by buying password keys at £3.50 a go. You
INFO ✓✓✓✓✓   need to download Adobe Acrobat Reader to view
VALUE ✓✓✓   the files.
EASE ✓✓✓

www.classicmotor.co.uk
CLASSIC CARS

ORIGIN UK
SPEED ✓✓✓
INFO ✓✓✓✓✓
VALUE ✓✓✓✓
EASE ✓✓

By far the best classic car site. It's comprehensive including clubs, classifieds and books; here you can buy anything from a car to a light bulb. It's not the easiest site to navigate though.

www.pistonheads.com
BEST OF BRITISH MOTORING

ORIGIN UK
SPEED ✓✓✓
INFO ✓✓✓✓✓
VALUE ✓✓✓
EASE ✓✓✓

Pistonheads is a British site dedicated to the faster side of motoring and is great for reviews of the latest cars. It's passionate and very informative.

www.cyberdrive.co.uk
PRACTISE FOR YOUR DRIVING TEST

ORIGIN UK
SPEED ✓✓✓
INFO ✓✓✓✓✓
VALUE ✓✓
EASE ✓✓✓

Brought to us by the Stationery Office, publishers of the Highway Code, this is an excellent way to learn and prepare for the real thing. £15 gets one month's complete access; you can take a virtual theory driving test which they'll mark and return your score.

For some more good advice try BSM's www.driving.co.uk or the very informative www.learners.co.uk, which has good links to related sites.

www.carquote.co.uk
CAR INSURANCE

ORIGIN UK
SPEED ✓✓✓
INFO ✓✓✓✓✓
VALUE ✓✓✓
EASE ✓✓✓

Quotes from a large number of insurance suppliers, you just fill in the form, and they get back to you with a quote. See also www.theaa.co.uk and www.eaglestar.co.uk.

Motorcycles

www.webbikes.co.uk
UK's PREMIER ON-LINE BIKING MAGAZINE

ORIGIN UK
SPEED ✓✓✓
INFO ✓✓✓✓✓
EASE ✓✓✓

News, bike features, chat, buying and selling, clubs, holidays and events are all covered in this well designed and informative site.

www.motorcycle.co.uk
THE UK's MOTORCYCLE DIRECTORY

ORIGIN UK
SPEED ✓✓✓
INFO ✓✓✓
EASE ✓✓✓✓

Essentially a list of links by brand, dealers, importers, classics, gear, books and auctions.
For more information on motorcycle clubs go to www.motorcycle.org.uk.

www.moto-directory.com
THE WORLD MOTORCYCLE DIRECTORY

ORIGIN US
SPEED ✓✓✓
INFO ✓✓✓✓✓
EASE ✓✓✓

US oriented, but links to 800 sites ensure that you'll know what's going on in motorcycling and find the information you need.

www.motorworld.com
ALL YOU NEED TO KNOW ABOUT MOTORCYCLES

ORIGIN US
SPEED ✓✓✓
INFO ✓✓✓✓
EASE ✓✓✓

Good coverage of both machines and events with multimedia features. Although the site is American there's a good British section. See also the better-designed www.bikenet.com.

Travel and Holidays

Travel is the biggest growth area on the internet, from holidays to insurance to local guides. If you're buying, then it definitely pays to shop around and try several sites, but be careful, it's amazing how fast the best deals are being snapped up. You may find that you still spend time on the phone, but the sites are constantly improving.

You could leave it to someone else to do the searching for you, at www.ybag.co.uk (page 171) you provide details of the holiday or trip you want and how much you're willing to pay, then they try to find a deal that will match your requirements.

The travel shops

www.expedia.co.uk
THE COMPLETE SERVICE

ORIGIN US/UK	This is the UK arm of Microsoft's very successful
SPEED ✓✓✓✓	on-line travel agency. It offers a huge array of holi-
INFO ✓✓✓✓✓	days, flights and associated services, for personal or
VALUE ✓✓✓	business, nearly all bookable on-line. It's easy and
EASE ✓✓✓	quicker than most, and there are some excellent

offers too. Not the trendiest but it's a good first stop. As with all the big operators, you have to register.

www.lastminute.com
DO SOMETHING LAST MINUTE

ORIGIN UK	This darling of the media is establishing an excellent
SPEED ✓✓	reputation not just as a travel agent, but as a
INFO ✓✓✓✓	good shopping site too. For travellers there is a
VALUE ✓✓✓✓	comprehensive sections on hotels, holidays and
EASE ✓✓✓✓	flights all with really good prices. There is also a

superb London restaurant guide and general entertainment section. You'll still have to phone the hotline for most holiday bookings.

www.thomascook.com
THE WIDEST RANGE OF PACKAGE HOLIDAYS

This site is easy-to-use and well laid out and, with

ORIGIN UK	over 2 million package holidays to chose from, you
SPEED ✓✓✓✓	should be able to find something to your liking. You
INFO ✓✓✓✓✓	can also browse the on-line magazine for ideas,
VALUE ✓✓✓✓	check the weather, search for cheap flights or holi-
EASE ✓✓✓✓	day deals; again you have to call the hotline to book.

www.its.net
INTERNET TRAVEL SERVICE

ORIGIN UK	An excellent place to start your search for travel
SPEED ✓✓✓✓	information or holidays with links classified into
INFO ✓✓✓✓✓	over 60 specialist sections.
EASE ✓✓✓✓✓	

Some other proven all round travel sites well worth checking out:

www.bargainholidays.com – Probably the best for quick breaks, excellent for late availability offers. It is linked to **www.travelocity.co.uk**, which is very fast and has good information on key destinations; excellent value.

www.e-bookers.com – Tedious to use, but good for Europe and flight deals.

http://new.leisureplanet.com – One stop holiday shop, everything on one site. Especially good for cruises, excellent quick search facility.

www.packageholidays.co.uk – Late bargain holidays and flights from over 130 tour operators includ-ing Thomson, Sunworld and Airtours.

www.leisurehunt.com – Great for hotels around the world, bookings can be made on-line.

www.balesworldwide.com – For something special, tailor-made holidays to the exotic parts of the world.

www.holidayauctions.net – Some bargains in the normal sense, and some flights and holidays you can bid for in the same way normal auctions work.

Airlines and flights only

www.cheapflights.co.uk
NOTHING BUT CHEAP FLIGHTS

ORIGIN UK
SPEED ✓✓✓
INFO ✓✓✓✓✓
VALUE ✓✓✓✓✓
EASE ✓✓✓

You don't need to register here to explore the great offers available from this site, but you still need to phone most of the travel agents or airlines listed to get your deal. See also **www.deckchair.com** which concentrates on getting value for money on flights, it can be a little slow but the results are usually worth it. They don't bother showing you the full priced fares.

For more cheap flight deals try these sites:

www.easyjet.co.uk – Great for a limited number of destinations, particularly good for UK flights.

www.ryanair.com – Very good for Ireland, northern Europe, Italy and France, clear and easy-to-use web site.

www.go-fly.com – From Stansted only but some excellent offers for Western Europe. Nicely designed site.

Travel information

www.travel.world.co.uk
FOR ALL YOUR TRAVEL REQUIREMENTS

ORIGIN UK
SPEED ✓✓✓
INFO ✓✓✓✓✓
EASE ✓✓✓

A massive, comprehensive site, it basically includes most available travel brochures with links to the relevant travel agent. It concentrates on Europe, so there are very few American sites but provides links to hotels, specialist holidays, cruises, self-catering and airlines. For a more global view go to **www.globalpassage.com** who offer 15,000 web sites to browse.

www.fco.gov.uk/travel
Advice from the Foreign Office

ORIGIN UK
SPEED ✓✓✓
INFO ✓✓✓✓✓
EASE ✓✓✓

Before you go get general advice, safety or visa information. For more travel safety information go to www.travelsafetytips.com.

www.tripprep.com
Travel health

ORIGIN US
SPEED ✓✓
INFO ✓✓✓✓
EASE ✓✓✓

A country-by-country risk assessment covering health, safety and politics; it can be a little out of date so check with the foreign office as well.

www.tips4trips.com
1000 tips for trips

ORIGIN UK
SPEED ✓✓✓
INFO ✓✓✓✓
EASE ✓✓✓✓

All the tips come from well meaning travellers and are categorised under sections such as pre-planning, what and how to pack, travelling for the disabled, for women, for men or with children.

www.webofculture.com/refs/gestures.html
Gestures of the world

ORIGIN US
SPEED ✓✓✓
INFO ✓✓✓✓
EASE ✓✓✓✓

Country-by-country, what their gestures mean, what not to do and what's best to do, all in a concise format.

www.vtourist.com
The Virtual Tourist

ORIGIN US
SPEED ✓✓✓
INFO ✓✓✓✓
EASE ✓✓✓

This allows you to explore destinations in a unique and fun way. Travellers describe their experiences, share photos, make recommendations and give tips so others benefit from their experience. See also www.travel-library.com which is less fun but combines recommendation with hard facts very well.

www.mytravelguide.com
ON-LINE TRAVEL GUIDES

ORIGIN US
SPEED ✓✓✓
INFO ✓✓✓✓✓
EASE ✓✓✓

A general American travel site that offers a good overview of most countries, with points of interest, very good interactive mapping and live web cams too. See also **http://city.net** which links to Excite's range of on-line travel guides.

www.gorp.com
FOR THE GREAT OUTDOORS

ORIGIN US
SPEED ✓✓✓
INFO ✓✓✓✓✓
EASE ✓✓✓

A great title, Gorp is dedicated to adventure, whether it be hiking, mountaineering, fishing, snow sports or riding the rapids. It is American, but is full of relevant good advice and information.

www.lonelyplanet.com
LONELY PLANET GUIDE

ORIGIN UK
SPEED ✓✓✓✓✓
INFO ✓✓✓✓✓
VALUE ✓✓✓✓
EASE ✓✓✓✓✓

A superb travel site, aimed at the independent traveller but with great information for everyone. Get a review on most world destinations or pick a theme and go with that, leave a message on the thorn tree, find out the latest news by country, get health reports and find out about the travel experiences of others – what's the real story? One of the best services is the eKno system, which is a combined phone, e-mail and answer machine which offers a great way to stay in touch when you're in the back of beyond.

http://travel.roughguides.com
ROUGH GUIDES

ORIGIN UK
SPEED ✓✓✓✓
INFO ✓✓✓✓✓
VALUE ✓✓✓
EASE ✓✓✓✓

Lively reviews on a huge number of places, by country and city as well as general travel information; you can share your travel thoughts with other travellers or buy a guide.

www.fodors.com
FODORS GUIDES

ORIGIN US	These guides give an American perspective, but
SPEED ✓	there is a huge amount of information on each
INFO ✓✓✓✓	destination. The site can be temperamental.
EASE ✓✓	

www.xe.net/currency
ON-LINE CURRENCY CONVERTER

ORIGIN US	The Universal Currency Converter could not be
SPEED ✓✓✓✓✓	easier to use, just select the currency you have, then
INFO ✓✓✓✓✓	the one you want to convert it to, press the button
EASE ✓✓✓✓✓	and you have your answer in seconds.

Destinations

www.antor.com
ASSOCIATION OF NATIONAL TOURIST OFFICES

ORIGIN UK	A useful start point to find information about some
SPEED ✓✓✓✓	90 countries that are members of the association,
INFO ✓✓✓✓	very good for links to key tourism sites.
EASE ✓✓✓✓	

www.indo.com
BALI ON-LINE

ORIGIN INDONESIA	Concentrating on Bali and its top hotels, but there's
SPEED ✓✓✓	also plenty of information on the rest of Indonesia
INFO ✓✓✓✓	as well as links to other Asian sites.
EASE ✓✓✓	

www.travelcanada.ca
EXPLORE CANADA

ORIGIN CANADA	Did you know that the glass floor at the top of the
SPEED ✓✓✓✓	world's tallest freestanding structure could support
INFO ✓✓✓✓✓	the weight of 14 large hippos? Find out much more
EASE ✓✓✓✓	at this wide-ranging and attractive site, from touring
	to city guides.

http://africa.com
AFRICA

ORIGIN S AFRICA
SPEED ✓✓✓✓✓
INFO ✓✓✓✓✓
EASE ✓✓✓✓

Exhaustive site covering news, information and travel in Africa, with very good country-by-country guides. See also www.ecoafrica.com and www.travelinafrica.co.za.

www.australia.com
DISCOVER AUSTRALIA

ORIGIN AUSTRALIA
SPEED ✓✓✓✓
INFO ✓✓✓✓
EASE ✓✓✓✓

The Australian Tourist Commission offer a good and informative site that gives lots of facts about the country, the people and their lifestyle and what you can expect when you visit.

www.franceway.com
VOILA LA FRANCE!

ORIGIN FRANCE
SPEED ✓✓✓✓
INFO ✓✓✓✓✓
EASE ✓✓✓✓

Excellent site giving an overview of French culture, history, facts and figures, and of course, how to book a holiday. You can also sign up for the newsletter. See also the official French Government Tourist office site www.francetourism.com.

www.germany-tourism.de
GERMANY – WUNDERBAR

ORIGIN GERMANY
SPEED ✓✓
INFO ✓✓✓✓✓
EASE ✓✓✓✓

As much information as you can handle with good features on the key destinations, excellent interactive map and links to related sites. For further information try www.germany-info.org.

www.gnto.gr
GREEK NATIONAL TOURIST ORGANISATION

ORIGIN GREECE
SPEED ✓✓✓✓
INFO ✓✓✓
EASE ✓✓✓✓

Attractive site with the official word on travelling in Greece, but some of the information is missing and the site is being reconstructed. Try **www.gogreece.com**, which is a search engine devoted to Greece, or the Greek Travel Pages at **www.gtpnet.com** who also have the latest ferry schedules for island hoppers.

www.indiamart.com
INDIA TRAVEL PROMOTION NETWORK

ORIGIN INDIA
SPEED ✓✓✓✓
INFO ✓✓✓✓✓
EASE ✓✓✓✓

A diverse mass of information including hotels, timetables, wildlife, worship, trekking, heritage and general tourism; it's well organised and easy-to-use. See also **www.india-travel.com** and **www.rrindia.com**.

www.emmeti.it
WELCOME TO ITALY

ORIGIN ITALY
SPEED ✓✓✓
INFO ✓✓✓✓
EASE ✓✓✓

A slightly eccentric site with bags of information, which is good, but takes a while to actually find. Very good for hotels, regional info and museums. See also **www.initaly.com**, an American site which is a little more organised.

www.shamrock.org
IRELAND

ORIGIN IRELAND
SPEED ✓✓✓✓
INFO ✓✓✓✓
EASE ✓✓✓✓

Wide ranging site giving you the best of Ireland. It really sells the country well, with good links to other related sites. See also **www.ireland-travel.ie**.

www.mideasttravelnet.com
MIDDLE EAST TRAVEL NETWORK

ORIGIN US
SPEED ✓✓✓
INFO ✓✓✓✓✓
EASE ✓✓✓✓

A well organised site concentrating on North Africa and the Middle East, easy-to-use, targeted slightly towards business users but still very useful for holiday-makers or independent travellers.

For good sites dedicated to individual Middle Eastern countries: http://touregypt.net, www.goisrael.com, www.jordan-online.com/travel.

www.purenz.com
NEW ZEALAND

ORIGIN NZ
SPEED ✓✓✓✓
INFO ✓✓✓✓
EASE ✓✓✓✓

Functional but informative site about the country, with a section devoted to the memories and recommendations from people who've visited. See also the comprehensive www.nz.com.

www.portugal-web.com

ORIGIN UK
SPEED ✓✓✓✓
INFO ✓✓✓✓✓
EASE ✓✓✓

A complete overview of the country including business as well as tourism, with good regional information, news and links to other related sites.

www.spaintour.com
TOURIST OFFICE OF SPAIN

ORIGIN SPAIN
SPEED ✓✓✓✓
INFO ✓✓✓✓✓
EASE ✓✓✓✓

A colourful and award winning web site that really makes you want to visit Spain. Very good for an overview but for in-depth information go to the sister site www.tourspain.es or try www.okspain.org.

www.go-unitedstates.com
A HIGHLIGHT IN EVERY STATE

ORIGIN US
SPEED ✓✓✓✓
INFO ✓✓✓✓
EASE ✓✓✓✓

Covers the USA by region, then state, with key destinations featured along with recommendations on where to stay, books to read and where to eat.

Travel Insurance

www.travelinsuranceclub.co.uk
AWARD WINNING TRAVEL INSURANCE CLUB

ORIGIN UK
SPEED ✓✓✓✓
INFO ✓✓✓✓
VALUE ✓✓✓✓
EASE ✓✓✓

Unfortunately there isn't one site for collating travel insurance yet, it's a question of shopping around. Here's a good place to start with a range of policies for backpackers, family and business travel.

All these companies offer flexibility and good value:

www.underthesun.co.uk – Good for annual and six monthly policies.

www.jameshampden.co.uk – Wide range of policies, straight forward and hassle free.

www.intersure.co.uk – Competitive.

www.columbusdirect.co.uk – Good information, nice web site and competitive prices.

On-line maps

www.mapquest.com
FINDING THE WAY

ORIGIN UK
SPEED ✓✓✓
INFO ✓✓✓✓✓
VALUE ✓✓✓
EASE ✓✓✓

Find out the best way to get from a to b in Europe or America. Not always as detailed as you'd like, but easy-to-use and you can customise your map or route plan. Good for information on the USA too.

www.multimap.com
COMPLETE INTERACTIVE ATLAS

ORIGIN UK
SPEED ✓✓✓
INFO ✓✓✓✓✓
EASE ✓✓✓✓✓

Easy-to-use, you can search using postcodes, London street names, place names or Ordnance Survey Grid reference. There's no route planner. For a similar site try www.streetmap.co.uk which is better for printing off maps, but doesn't drill down as far.

www.mapsonus.com
NAVIGATE THE USA

ORIGIN US	It's notoriously difficult to find your way around
SPEED ✓✓✓	America, but by using the route planner you should
INFO ✓✓✓✓	minimise your risk of getting lost.
EASE ✓✓✓✓	

Britain

www.visitbritain.com
HOME OF THE BRITISH TOURIST AUTHORITY

ORIGIN UK	Selling Britain using a holiday ideas-led site with
SPEED ✓✓✓	lots of help for the visitor, maps, background stories,
INFO ✓✓✓✓✓	images, entertainment, culture, activities and a
EASE ✓✓✓✓	planner. There's also a very helpful set of links.

www.informationbritain.co.uk
HOLIDAY INFORMATION

ORIGIN UK	Where to stay and where to go with an overview of
SPEED ✓✓✓	all the UK's main tourist attractions, counties and
INFO ✓✓✓✓✓	regions, it has good cross-referencing and links to
EASE ✓✓✓✓	the major destinations.

www.atuk.co.uk
UK TRAVEL AND TOURIST GUIDE

ORIGIN US	A good county-by-county guide with plenty of
SPEED ✓✓✓	extras such as web cams, awards, weather, site of
INFO ✓✓✓✓✓	the day and competitions. It's very good if you want
EASE ✓✓✓	something unusual. See also www.aboutbritain.com.

www.travelbritain.com
TOURS

ORIGIN UK	Primarily a site geared to selling tours, but there is a
SPEED ✓✓✓✓	great deal of unusual information about everything
INFO ✓✓✓✓✓	from adults only to hunting ghosts.
EASE ✓✓✓	

www.ni-tourism.com
NORTHERN IRELAND TOURIST BOARD

ORIGIN UK
SPEED ✓✓✓✓✓
INFO ✓✓✓✓✓
EASE ✓✓✓✓

An attractive site showing the best that Northern Ireland has to offer, with a virtual tour, holiday planner, accommodation, guides and special offers.

www.a2btravel.co.uk
BOOKING BRITAIN

ORIGIN UK
SPEED ✓✓✓
INFO ✓✓✓✓✓
EASE ✓✓✓✓

Acknowledged as the best on-line travel information and booking service for the UK. The site offers the ability to book rooms in over 33,000 hotels, inns and guesthouses. There are other services such as travel tips, airport guides, ferry information plus links to specialist sister sites giving a more holistic travel service.

www.laterooms.co.uk
HOTEL INDUSTRY LATE AVAILABILITY DATABASE

ORIGIN UK
SPEED ✓✓✓
INFO ✓✓✓✓✓
EASE ✓✓✓✓

An attempt to fill empty beds, all you do is enter a destination and length of stay, then a selection appears. Works about two weeks ahead. You can also search by hotel type as well just look at the biggest savings or best deals. There are also sections for USA and European destinations.

www.londontown.com
OFFICIAL SITE FOR LONDON

ORIGIN UK
SPEED ✓✓
INFO ✓✓✓✓✓
EASE ✓✓✓✓

A survival and holiday guide rolled into one, with sections on restaurants, hotels, attractions and offers. It is quite slow.

www.nationaltrust.org.uk
PLACES OF HISTORIC INTEREST AND BEAUTY

ORIGIN UK
SPEED ✓✓✓✓
INFO ✓✓✓✓✓
EASE ✓✓✓✓✓

The National Trust's site has an excellent overview of their activities and the properties they own. There is a very good search facility and up to date information to help with your visit.

www.knowhere.co.uk
THE USER'S GUIDE TO BRITAIN

ORIGIN UK
SPEED ✓✓✓✓
INFO ✓✓✓✓✓
EASE ✓✓✓✓

An unconventional "tourist guide" which gives a warts and all account of over 1000 places in Britain; it's very irreverent and if you are squeamish or a bit sensitive then they have a good list of links to proper tourist sites.

www.theaa.co.uk
AUTOMOBILE ASSOCIATION

ORIGIN UK
SPEED ✓✓✓✓
INFO ✓✓✓✓✓
EASE ✓✓✓✓✓

A superb site that is divided into four key sections; breakdown cover, route planning and traffic information, hotel guide and booking, and help with buying a car. There is also information on insurance and other financial help.

www.rac.co.uk
GET AHEAD WITH THE RAC

ORIGIN UK
SPEED ✓✓✓
INFO ✓✓✓✓✓
EASE ✓✓✓✓

Great for UK traffic reports and has a very reliable route planner. There's also a good section on finding the right place to stay, and lots of help if you want to buy a car.

Train, coach and ferry journeys

www.railtrack.co.uk
FOR TRAIN TIMES

ORIGIN UK
SPEED ✓✓✓
INFO ✓✓✓✓✓
EASE ✓✓✓

Go to the travel section and type in the start point and destination then Railtrack will tell you the time of the next train. It's very easy-to-use and must for all rail travellers. You can also get travel news and information about Railtrack but there's no details of rail fares.

www.thetrainline.com
BUY TRAIN TICKETS

ORIGIN UK
SPEED ✓✓✓
INFO ✓✓✓✓✓
VALUE ✓✓✓
EASE ✓✓✓✓

You can book a ticket for train travel, whether business or leisure, (except sleeper, Motorail, Eurostar and ferry services) they have an up-to-date timetable and the tickets will be sent or you can collect.

www.ferrysavers.co.uk
BOOKING FERRY CROSSINGS

ORIGIN UK
SPEED ✓✓✓
INFO ✓✓✓✓✓
VALUE ✓✓✓
EASE ✓✓✓✓

For cars only at time of going to press, you can book for Boulogne, Calais, Eurotunnel, Ostend and Dieppe as well as Dublin and Rosslare. Some discounts are available.

www.nationalexpress.co.uk
BOOK COACH TICKETS

ORIGIN US
SPEED ✓✓✓
INFO ✓✓✓✓✓
EASE ✓✓✓

Organise your journey with this easy-to-use web site, then book the tickets. Also offers an airport service, transport to events and tours.

Utilities

Electricity & gas

www.hydro.co.uk

SCOTTISH HYDRO ELECTRIC

ORIGIN UK
SPEED ✓✓✓✓
INFO ✓✓✓✓
VALUE ✓✓✓
EASE ✓✓✓✓

Not the best looking site, but the most customer oriented of the major energy companies, with obvious links to the various offers and areas of help.

Other energy company sites geared to customers are:

www.london-electricity.co.uk – straight forward, easy-to-use.

www.easternenergy.co.uk – good service, but slow site.

www.gas.co.uk – comprehensive service.

Listed below are the other electricity and gas companies, sadly the sites tend to be corporate and the customer is a bit of an afterthought.

www.british-energy.com – The largest electricity provider, also trading as Swalec – **www.swalec.co.uk**.

www.meb.co.uk – Midland Electricity.

www.ngc.co.uk – The National Grid.

www.nie.co.uk – Northern Ireland Electricity.

www.national-power.com – the customer section is under "energy services".

www.centrica.co.uk – owners of British Gas and the AA.

www.transco.uk.com

FOR GAS LEAKS

ORIGIN UK
SPEED ✓✓✓✓
INFO ✓✓✓
EASE ✓✓✓✓

Transco doesn't sell gas, but maintains the 24-hour emergency service for stopping gas leaks – call 0800 111 999 to report one.

www.corgi-gas.co.uk
COUNCIL FOR REGISTERED GAS INSTALLERS

ORIGIN UK
SPEED ✓✓✓✓
INFO ✓✓✓✓
EASE ✓✓✓✓

CORGI is the gas industry watchdog; the site has advice on gas installation and where to find a fitter or repairman.

Water

www.nww.co.uk
NORTH WEST WATER

ORIGIN UK
SPEED ✓✓✓✓
INFO ✓✓✓✓
EASE ✓✓✓✓

NWW has the best-designed site with help, information and good advice for consumers, with on-line access to your account.

All these water suppliers offer more corporate sites:
www.severn-trent.com
www.swwater.co.uk
www.wessexwater.plc.uk.

The Weather

www.met-office.gov.uk
EXCELLING IN WEATHER SERVICES

ORIGIN UK
SPEED ✓✓
INFO ✓✓✓✓✓
EASE ✓✓✓✓

Comprehensive information on Britain's favourite topic of conversation. It is easy-to-use with the emphasis on education and has a good selection of related links. Provides 3-day and long-range forecasts by region, city or for the whole country. Check the weather and pressure charts, satellite images for the rest of the world as well.

www.bbc.co.uk/weather
ANOTHER WINNER FROM THE BBC

ORIGIN UK

SPEED ✓✓✓✓

INFO ✓✓✓✓✓

EASE ✓✓✓✓

Another page from the BBC site that gives up-to-the-minute forecasts, it is very clear and concise. It features:

1. Five-day forecasts for 105 towns and cities.
2. Ski reports, sun index, world weather and the shipping forecast.
3. A section dedicated to weather-related articles.
4. Details on making the weather forecast program.
    For more information about the weather, the Weather Channel has a very good site on www.weather.com. US biased but interesting.

www.weatherimages.org
SEE THE WORLD'S WEATHER – LIVE

ORIGIN US

SPEED ✓✓

INFO ✓✓✓✓

EASE ✓✓✓✓

Weatherimages is compiled by an amateur weather fan. Split into about twenty informative sections, the best feature is the Weather Cams, from which you can see the world's weather from the Antarctic to Northern Europe via Bondi beach or Rio.

Web Cameras

One of the most fascinating aspects of the internet is the ability to tap into some CCTV or specially set up web cameras from all around the world.

www.I-spy.com
THE MOTHER OF ALL WEB CAM DIRECTORIES

ORIGIN US

SPEED ✓

INFO ✓✓✓✓

EASE ✓✓✓✓

A directory of over 3000 sites, and a great starting out point to the world of web cam. Easy-to-use but as with all these sites you need patience.

Wine

see Food and Drink

Web site guides/directories

Odd though it may be for a web site guide to recommend other web site guides these sites are well worth investigating.

http://cool.infi.net
THE COOLEST SITES

ORIGIN	US	Vote for the coolest sites, and find out which are
SPEED	✓✓✓	considered the best.
INFO	✓✓✓✓✓	
EASE	✓✓✓	

www.ukdirectory.co.uk
DEFINITIVE GUIDES TO BRITISH SITES

ORIGIN	US	A massive database of web sites conveniently
SPEED	✓✓✓	categorised into 14 sections, it's mainly geared to
INFO	✓✓✓✓✓	business, but there's leisure too. They don't review,
EASE	✓✓✓	but there are brief explanations.

See also **www.website-directory.co.uk**.

Weddings

www.confetti.co.uk
YOUR INTERACTIVE WEDDING GUIDE

ORIGIN	UK	Designed to help you through every stage of your
SPEED	✓✓✓✓	wedding with information for all participants. There
INFO	✓✓✓✓✓	are gift guides, planning tools, advice, a supplier
VALUE	✓✓✓	directory and a shop. They don't miss much.
EASE	✓✓✓✓	

www.all-about-weddings.co.uk

INFORMATION ABOUT GETTING MARRIED IN THE UK

ORIGIN UK
SPEED ✓✓✓
INFO ✓✓✓✓✓
VALUE ✓✓✓
EASE ✓✓✓✓

Excellent for basic information about weddings, from initial planning, to the ceremony and the reception; it also has an excellent set of links to related and specialist supplier sites. See also **www.hitched.co.uk** who offer a similar service, but with a bit more fun.

Women

www.handbag.com

THE ISP FOR WOMEN

ORIGIN UK
SPEED ✓✓✓✓
INFO ✓✓✓✓✓
VALUE ✓✓✓
EASE ✓✓✓✓

Described as the most useful place on the internet for British women, it has a mass of information, links and shopping. For some it's a little too commercial though. For a more magazine-style approach try **www.icircle.co.uk**, it's part of the Freeserve network, calling itself the Women's Channel.

www.women.com

THE SMART WAY TO GET THINGS DONE

ORIGIN US
SPEED ✓✓✓
INFO ✓✓✓✓✓
EASE ✓✓✓✓

Aimed at the professional American woman this is a no nonsense site offering a great deal of news, information and recommendation on a wide variety of topics. See also **www.womenswire.com** and **www.webgrrls.com** both of who offer similar information but in differing styles.

www.journeywoman.com

PREMIER TRAVEL RESOURCE FOR WOMEN

ORIGIN US
SPEED ✓✓✓
INFO ✓✓✓✓✓
VALUE ✓✓✓
EASE ✓✓✓✓

Dedicated to ensuring safe travel for women, registering gets you access to the free newsletter plus lots of advice, guidance and tips. For another good but US biased site try **www.women-traveling.com**.

www.winmagazine.org
WOMEN'S INTERNATIONAL NET

ORIGIN US ✓✓✓
SPEED ✓✓✓
INFO ✓✓✓✓
EASE ✓✓✓✓

This is an on-line magazine devoted to bringing together women from all over the world for dialogue and mutual understanding. Some of the writing is excellent, but it can be a little dull.

Stop Press

The World Wide Web continually move on and we've added this section to catch sites that we missed in the first draft. All are good and will be fully reviewed in the next edition – The Good Web Site Guide 2002.

Art – posters

www.barewall.com The internet's largest art and print store, excellent but beware the shipping costs.

Booksellers

http://bookshop.blackwell.co.uk Blackwells are best known for academic and professional books, but their site offers much more, with the emphasis on recommendation and help finding the right book.

www.borders.com A bookseller just making in-roads into the UK offering a site that is heavily US biased, but great for something different. Good offers on books, music and DVD, though shipping is comparatively expensive.

Dictionaries

www.oed.com Costs £350 for on-line usage.

Education

www.learnfree.co.uk Excellent resource for parents, covering the National Curriculum and much more.
www.homeworkhigh.com Well-designed homework help site from Channel 4.

Fashion

www.lookfantastic.com Everything a girl needs – it's war out there.

Finance

www.virtuallyanywhere.co.uk Your local store of financial advisers – good for tax.

Gardening

www.dig-it.co.uk Beautifully designed garden shop and magazine.
www.crocus.co.uk For the whole gardening experience, another good looking site full of ideas.
www.greenfingers.com Good for gardening advice and information, with a well priced shop.
www.glut.co.uk The Gluttonous Gardener provides presents for every gardener. It's a bit short on information though.

Health

www.thinknatural.com A mass of information on every aspect of natural health, there's also a very comprehensive shop.

Movies

www.filmunlimited.co.uk A movie site from the *Guardian*, it's exceptional because of its links and trailer service.

News

www.newsplayer.com Relive the events of the past hundred years; witness them first hand as they happened. A truly superb site with £25 a year subscription fee.

Property

www.bambooavenue.com Moving help, advice and service quotes.

Search Engine

www.directhit.com Excellent answer to specific questions and detailed searches.

Shopping

www.priceoffers.co.uk The on-line guide to high street bargains, check out the site then choose which supermarkets to visit for the best offers.

Teenagers

www.teensites.org Everything a teenager wants – on one site, but with an American bias.

Telecommunications

www.mediaring.com Excellent internet voice communications products, good value too.

Transport – cars

www.tins.co.uk Buy your next car on-line. Not the cheapest but they have a huge selection to choose from.

Travel

www.netflights.com The Airline Network – great for cheap flights and more.

Travel – Britain

www.goodbeachguide.co.uk Find out which are the best and worst beaches.

www.aboutbritain.com A great overview of tourist Britain, what's in and where to go. See also www.enjoybritain.com for links to other key tourist sites.

www.gardenvisit.com Gardens to visit alongside an excellent overview of garden history.

www.sightseeing.co.uk A quick and easy-to-use UK tourism site, it's excellent if you're stuck for something to do.

Travel – maps

www.mapblast.com Get a detailed map and information on virtually anywhere.

www.easymap.co.uk Superb interactive map of the UK.

For Women

www.beme.com Beautifully designed women's magazine site with loads of goodies.